Inside Front Cover ➤

CILANTRO

P. J. BIROSIK

COLLIER BOOKS
Macmillan Publishing Company
NEW YORK

Maxwell Macmillan Canada
TORONTO

Maxwell Macmillan International
NEW YORK   OXFORD   SINGAPORE   SYDNEY

Collier Books
Macmillan Publishing Company
866 Third Avenue
New York, NY 10022

Maxwell Macmillan Canada, Inc.
1200 Eglinton Avenue East
Suite 200
Don Mills, Ontario M3C 3N1

Macmillan Publishing Company is part of the Maxwell Communication Group of Companies.

Library of Congress Cataloging-in-Publication Data
Birosik, Patti Jean.
Cilantro/P.J. Birosik.—1st Collier Books ed.
p.   cm.
Includes index.
ISBN 0-02-016605-2
1. Cookery (Coriander)   I. Title.
TX819.C65B57   1994
641.6'57—dc20   93-46064
CIP

Macmillan books are available at special discounts for bulk purchases for sales promotions,
premiums, fund-raising, or educational use. For details, contact:

Special Sales Director
Macmillan Publishing Company
866 Third Avenue
New York, NY 10022

Cover photographs by David Bishop
Food Styling by Mariann Sauvion

Illustrations by Jill Karla Schwarz

Book Design by Michael Mendelsohn
of MM Design 2000, Inc.

First Collier Books Edition 1994

10   9   8   7   6   5   4   3   2   1

Printed in the United States of America

Happy are those who dream dreams
and have the courage to make them come true.

CONTENTS

ACKNOWLEDGMENTS

Sincere thanks (and a big Huzzah!) to my editor, Justin Schwartz, and agent, Madeleine Morel, for their enthusiasm and effort on behalf of this work; three cheers to Patricia Stewart of the Sedona Public Library for her endless good humor and nudges in the right direction, particularly during the historical research phase; a big pat on the back to Executive Sous Chef William R. Leroux III, of the Los Abrigados resort, for helping to perfect the frozen dessert recipes; and, as always, gratitude to my friends and family for their encouragement during the trial-and-(t)error experiments as well as their finger-lickin' appreciation when the recipes turned out right. The Macmillan/Collier staff also deserve applause, for the book you hold in your hands exists only because many people worked hard to make it not only available but lovely and readable. As with a fine meal, attention to detail is all, and sincerest efforts yield the most joyous results.

INTRODUCTION

Cilantro is not only my favorite green, it is also the most used herb in the world! It is available around the globe under the names *coriander* (Europe), *Chinese parsley* (Asia), *fresh coriander* (India and the Middle East), and *cilantro* (the Americas). Its bright, lemon-soapy flavor may be an acquired taste to some, but when used correctly in recipes, this delicately fragrant plant can impart an irresistibly subtle nuance or appealingly robust overtone to all manner of meat, fish, fowl, and vegetables.

The most versatile of herbs, cilantro possesses both tender, edible stalks and fragile, fringed leaves; its dried seeds can be found in virtually any kitchen spice collection and are used in the commercial preparation of hot dogs, candy, smoking tobacco, pickles, vermouth, and gin. This book emphasizes use of the fresh plant, though several tantalizing recipes feature both leaves and seeds, and one historic cookie recipe from colonial America has been included to demonstrate the herb's enduring popularity.

In addition to being a culinary staple worldwide, fresh coriander is prized for its medicinal and beautifying properties. The herb is a vital ingredient in spring tonics, soothing and clarifying facial masks, enriching hair conditioners, perfumes, and invigorating herbal baths. I have even seen the feathery stalks used to counterpoint small orchids in flower arrangements!

In the early 1800s, dried coriander seeds were combined with cloves, cinnamon bark, oak shavings, and crushed rose petals in small linen or muslin bags and hung in wardrobes or folded into drawers to keep clothes from smelling musty. A few decades later, the fresh herb's leaves were crushed with rosemary stalks, lavender

flowers, and a little olive oil into a liniment pack to be placed on the scalp; if used regularly, the concoction was thought to promote hair growth.

Herbs have been used throughout history to cure ills and enhance good health; *Apocrypha: Ecclesiasticus, xxxviii*, 4 states: "The Lord hath created medicines out of the earth; and he that is wise will not abhor them." Taking this to heart, the modern herbal health movement has developed many tonics, one of which combines ginseng root, damiana, astragalus, star anise, and coriander seed with burgundy or chardonnay for a "long life wine." While a daily tablespoon dose is recommended, many have found the herbed vintage irresistibly delicious and imbibe entire glassfuls!

While you won't find a recipe for cilantro spirits herein, I'm sure you will discover many other equally enticing culinary adventures that will turn an average meal into a cilantro celebration. I wish you much fun and good eating!

ABOUT CILANTRO

FORMAL DEFINITION AND DESCRIPTION

Coriander (*Coriandrum sativum*, of the Umbelliferae family)—a herbaceous annual related to parsley, dill, and cumin; it's cultivated for its tiny, fragrant fruits (coriander seeds), which ripen from a small spray of flowers, and for its tender, frilly leaves.

Records of use date back to 5000 B.C., making it one of the earliest herbs known to have been used by man. The herb is also mentioned in the book of Exodus; as the Children of Israel made their long trek to the Promised Land, they were nourished by *manna* "which was as coriander seed . . . and the people went about, and gathered it in, grinding it in mills, or beating it in mortars, then baking it in pans and making cakes of it."

The herb is rumored to have been grown in the Hanging Gardens of Babylon, was placed in Egyptian tombs over three thousand years ago, and is among medicinal plants mentioned in the Medical Papyrus of Thebes (written in 1552 B.C.).

Ancient Greeks and Romans favored it as a bread flavoring, allowing the seeds to ripen before being used whole or ground. Asian, Latin American, and other cultures have historically utilized only fresh leaves; no recipe calling for dried cilantro leaves has been found by this author.

The plant is native to the Mediterranean and Caucasus regions and is extensively cultivated in India, Asia Minor, Morocco, and parts of Europe. It is also grown in the United States, where the plant has escaped cultivation and now grows wild; this expansion currently includes parts of Mexico and Central and South America. Spanish and Portuguese explorers, as well as Catholic missionaries, are believed to

have brought the herb with them to the New World, where it was planted as part of extensive herb and vegetable gardens at newly established settlements.

The plant's finely grooved, extremely slender, hollow stems spring from a thin, spindly-shaped root and grow to a height of one to three feet (thirty to ninety centimeters), but are rarely utilized for culinary purposes. The herb has bipinnate leaves and small flowers in pink or whitish umbels; the intriguing taste of the leaves has been described fondly as a blend of lemon and sage, while those who dislike it claim it's flavored like lemony soap.

The fruits, or seeds, are two semiglobular bodies joined on the commissural, or inner, sides (a schizocarp), giving the appearance of a single, smooth, nearly globular fruit about two tenths of an inch (five millimeters) in diameter; they have a white to yellowish brown color and a mild, fragrant aroma.

Coriander seeds are a principal ingredient in curries, sausages, pickles, liqueurs, Scandinavian pastries, and confectioneries such as English *comfits* (old-fashioned pink or white candies with a hard sugar shell formed around coriander seed). Coriander leaves, more popularly known as *cilantro*, are a principal ingredient in salsa, chutney, sauces, pestos, and salads. The plant's essential oils are used in beverages, candies, tobacco, and perfumes, as well as to disguise the unpleasant taste of some medicines.

In Canton, China, both leaves and seeds are used to help remove unpleasant odors occurring in the groin area of both men and women; this Chinese remedy is also a cure for bad breath—six tablespoons of coriander seed are added to three quarts of rapidly boiling water, which is then simmered for two to three hours or until the mixture has been reduced to less than a quart of water. Whole coriander leaves, grated orange peel, and a dash of peppermint oil are added, and the mixture is removed from heat and left to steep for an hour. Once strained into a container and sealed, the liquid can be used as a mouth rinse or sponged onto the groin and left to air dry. It is stored in a sealed container in the refrigerator. A second Cantonese

apothecary recommended the steeping of fresh parsley in addition to the cilantro, while a third recommended wintergreen oil as a more effective alternative to oil of peppermint.

CHOOSING AND STORING FRESH CILANTRO

Cilantro is readily available in supermarkets and specialty produce shops under the names *cilantro*, *fresh coriander*, *coriander*, and *Chinese parsley* all year round. It is sold in bunches in the vegetable section, usually next to parsley or watercress. It can be identified from these other bunched greens by its lighter green color, extremely thin stalks, and feathery frilled leaves. If in doubt, pluck a leaf and chew it; it should have a bright lemony flavor.

Organic cilantro is best, as some commercial chemical fertilizers leach or otherwise alter the delicate characteristic flavor of the herb. If the sampled leaf has no flavor, do not purchase the bunch; likewise, if the leaf has a bitter flavor, disregard it and sample-taste other leaves in another bunch. Cilantro should never be kept on ice, nor should it be overwatered once placed on display; repeated washing from overhead spray jets can often damage the integrity of the leaves, leaving them with a watery flavor and limp texture. Choose an herb bunch underneath the top layer of displayed produce, if possible; in some climates, overenthusiastic air-conditioning can also damage this delicate plant, forcing its distinctive aromatic oils to leach out.

Avoid cilantro with many brown or brown-edged leaves; this indicates that the plant has suffered wind damage. Also disregard bunches with numerous yellow leaves; these are signs of overwatering prior to harvesting. The perfect bunch of cilantro has resilient, fine-limbed stalks with elastic, bright green leaves; no leaf fringe should be dry or mottled in color. Do not buy a cilantro bunch that is pale green overall; this is an immature plant and will not possess much flavor.

Buy only the amount of cilantro you will be using within a twenty-four-hour

period for peak flavor and texture. Store fresh cilantro in a sealed plastic bag in the refrigerator for up to three days for good flavor; if the herb is to be used in soup or stew, it may be kept for an additional twenty-four hours. It is advisable, but not required, to soak a paper towel in cool water and wrap it around the bottom two inches of the stems prior to placing the bunch in the bag. It is not recommended to leave this herb exposed in the refrigerator; cilantro has a tendency to dry out or wilt when exposed to constantly changing temperatures due to refrigerator doors being opened and closed, and it can also be tainted by the aromas of strong-smelling vegetables such as onions, shallots, leeks, scallions, and chili peppers, as well as by fish.

Cilantro should not be frozen and is not used in a dried form.

HANDLING TIPS FOR FRESH CILANTRO

Wash cilantro after separating the bunch into small bouquets. Place each bouquet under a gentle stream (or, preferably, a light spray) of cool—not cold!—running water and shake gently, turning the entire bouquet 360 degrees to rinse off any debris and to avoid bruising the leaves. Do not use warm or hot water as this may wilt the herb. After rinsing, arrange bouquets on a flat paper towel and let air dry at room temperature; you may also cover the damp bouquets with a second paper towel and tap gently to dislodge water drops from leaves, but DO NOT PRESS DOWN!

You will be tempted to pull cilantro leaves off their stalk, but resist. If pulled, the leaves often bring with them a thin thread, similar to a celery string, that invariably gets stuck between teeth. Remember that the leaves are very thin and bruise easily, so minimal handling is best. Grasp the bottom end of individual stalks and snip off leaves where they connect to stems with a small pair of kitchen shears or manicure scissors. Discard stems unless recipe calls for them.

When using both leaves and stems, chop off and discard the lower third of stalks while the cilantro is still wrapped in its original bunch; the lower part of stalks

can be woody in texture and rather earthy tasting. Wash and dry cilantro as described above before proceeding to process the herb as is called for in your recipe.

GROWING CILANTRO FROM SEED

This is a popular, easy-to-grow annual possessing both edible leaves and usable fruits (or seeds) that can be safely consumed by both humans and animals. Note: as with all parsley, this plant is not recommended for parrots or hookbills in either raw or cooked states.

Select a sunny location with very well drained, friable soil that is alkaline (or "sweet"); sow seeds only when all danger of frost is past and firm soil over the seeds. Cultivate the soil and enrich it regularly with vegetable food fertilizer; protect plants from wind as it withers the extremely tender leaves, leaving them brown, dry, and inedible. This herb does not transplant well.

Planting depth:	½" (13 mm)
Seed spacing:	1" (3 cm)
Spacing between rows:	15" (38 cm)
Days to germination:	15 to 20
Spacing after thinning:	8" (20 cm), at 25 to 30 days
Days to maturity:	65 to 75

When ready to harvest, gather seeds as they are ripening and let dry indoors; seeds may be used whole or crushed. Pick leaves sparingly as plants grow, or wait until maturity and cut off entire stalks; fresh leaves may be used whole or chopped.

APPETIZERS

SALMON-CILANTRO SPREAD ON MELBA ROUNDS

Whether you need an instant appetizer for unexpected guests, a simple game-time snack, or a light lunch, this sensational spread is as delicious as it is versatile. For a tray of intriguingly attractive canapés, top each spoonful of spread with a red or green pepper strip, chopped green onion, or sliced black olive; it can also be used to fill celery stalks. The spread's consistency should be fairly smooth and well integrated.

1 cup cooked salmon, flaked (and drained, if canned)
¾ cup cilantro leaves
1 tablespoon chopped white onion
1 tablespoon fresh-squeezed lemon juice
1 tablespoon mayonnaise
½ teaspoon prepared mustard
24 melba rounds or other type cracker

Place salmon, cilantro leaves, and onion into a food processor. Mix at medium speed for 30 seconds. Add the lemon juice, mayo, and mustard. Mix at high speed for 1 minute or until the mixture is fairly smooth. Slather each melba round with the spread and place on serving platter. Serve immediately.

MAKES ABOUT 6 SERVINGS.

SALSA FRESCA

Using only the freshest ingredients, this extremely versatile marinated salsa makes the perfect topping for barbecued meats, broiled chicken, grilled hamburgers, and boiled hot dogs. It can be stirred into soups or stews, ladled onto linguine or angel hair pasta, and served with chips or vegetable sticks as a low-calorie dip. As given below, the serrano chilis give the finished product a medium-hot finish; for less fire-power, use fewer peppers.

8 roma tomatoes, seeded and diced into ½-inch cubes
½ medium red onion, diced into ¼-inch cubes
4 serrano chili peppers, seeded and minced
½ cup chopped cilantro leaves
2 tablespoons fresh lemon juice
½ teaspoon oregano
½ teaspoon salt
½ teaspoon sugar

Combine the tomatoes, onion, peppers, and cilantro leaves in a medium bowl. Combine the lemon juice, oregano, salt, and sugar in a small bowl and mix well. Pour the lemon mixture over the tomato mixture. Toss and serve immediately for best flavor; it can be covered and refrigerated, but should be used within 24 hours.

MAKES APPROXIMATELY 2 CUPS, 2 TO 4 SERVINGS.

CILANTRO CANAPÉ SPREAD

This rich, smoky spread should be presented in a small bowl surrounded by crackers and little plates of sliced black olives, minced green and red bell pepper, mini-scallion sprigs (cut off roots and 6 inches of green top, then split onion in half lengthwise), diced pimiento, and finely chopped red onion. Guests can customize their crackers as they wish; they can also use this spread to stuff celery sticks.

6 ounces smoked baby Swiss, diced
3 ounces cream cheese, sliced
¼ cup finely chopped cilantro leaves
2 tablespoons mayonnaise
1 tablespoon milk
1 teaspoon grated lemon zest

Place all the ingredients in a food processor. Process on low speed until just blended. Spoon the spread into a serving bowl and serve immediately, or cover and serve within 24 hours.

MAKES ABOUT 1 CUP, 4 TO 8 SERVINGS.

CILANTRO–SOUR CREAM DIP

Creamy and luxurious, this smooth-as-silk chip dip can also be used to dunk crudités; try serving it alongside raw broccoli florets and jícama and zucchini spears as an alternative to the usual carrot and celery sticks. Thinned even further by the addition of 2 to 3 tablespoons of buttermilk, this dip transforms into a rich salad dressing.

1 cup sour cream
Two 3-ounce packages of cream cheese, sliced
¾ cup finely chopped cilantro leaves
1 tablespoon finely diced white onion
½ teaspoon salt (optional)
½ teaspoon freshly grated lemon zest
¼ teaspoon cayenne powder
Garnish:
2 thin slices red radish
1 small cilantro sprig

Place all the ingredients in a food processor. Process on low speed until well blended, being careful not to liquefy. Pour dip into a serving bowl and garnish with radish and cilantro sprigs. Serve immediately.

MAKES 1 CUP, 4 TO 8 SERVINGS.

MEXICAN MEATBALLS

Simmered in salsa, these ground beef or lamb meatballs make a heady alternative to the customary Swedish buffet mainstay. To turn this dish into an enticing entrée, serve in a nest of linguine with extra sauce on the side to smother the noodles.

4 large tomatoes, seeded and chopped
2 poblano chili peppers, blackened, skinned, seeded, and chopped
¼ cup water
¼ cup chopped yellow onion
1 clove garlic, minced
¼ cup minced cilantro leaves
1 teaspoon sugar
1 teaspoon salt
1 ½ pounds ground beef (lamb may be substituted)
½ cup finely chopped yellow onion
¼ cup finely chopped cilantro leaves
¼ cup fine dry bread crumbs
1 garlic clove, minced
½ teaspoon freshly ground black pepper
½ teaspoon salt
3 tablespoons canola oil

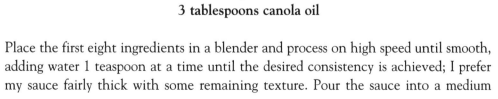

Place the first eight ingredients in a blender and process on high speed until smooth, adding water 1 teaspoon at a time until the desired consistency is achieved; I prefer my sauce fairly thick with some remaining texture. Pour the sauce into a medium

saucepan and warm over low heat, stirring occasionally. Combine the next seven ingredients in a large bowl and mix until thoroughly blended. Shape into 1-inch balls. Heat the oil in large skillet over medium-high heat. Fry the meatballs for 5 to 6 minutes, turning frequently, or until a sampled meatball is browned and no longer pink in the middle. Remove the meatballs with a slotted spoon and drain on paper towels. Place drained meatballs in a chafing dish. Pour sauce over meatballs and serve immediately.

MAKES APPROXIMATELY 24 MEATBALLS, OR 6 SERVINGS.

SALADS

CILANTRO AND CUCUMBER NOODLES IN ASPIC

This magnificent molded salad boasts plenty of citrus zest, with the added attraction of *cucumber noodles*. Your family will love puzzling over this ingredient, but let's keep the preparation our little secret, okay? Serve this item as a separate course for formal dinners, or slice it onto plates brimming with picnic fare; it makes a spectacular buffet centerpiece, too!

1 cup water
2 tablespoons fresh-squeezed lemon juice
One 3-ounce package of lemon gelatin
1 cup cold water
¼ teaspoon salt
1 medium cucumber, peeled
1 cup cilantro leaves
1 carrot, shaved
2 tablespoons freshly grated lemon zest
2 tablespoons freshly grated orange zest
Garnish:
1 bunch cilantro, sectioned into sprigs

Boil the water and lemon juice in a small pot over high heat. Remove from the heat. Pour in the gelatin and dissolve thoroughly. Add cold water and salt. Pour the gelatin mixture into 3-cup mold. Place in the refrigerator and chill until partially set,

about 30 minutes. While the gelatin is setting, cut the cucumber in half lengthwise. Scrape out and discard seeds. Slice the cucumber halves in the middle. Cut each cucumber piece into long thin strips about ⅛-inch wide. Lay thin strips flat and slice into narrow noodle shapes, about ⅛-inch thick (think fettuccine). In a large bowl, combine the cucumber noodles, cilantro, carrot, and zests. Remove the gelatin from refrigerator and stir in the cucumber mixture, distributing evenly. Return to the refrigerator and chill until firm, at least 2 hours. To unmold the salad, fill the sink with hot water. Dip the mold into hot water, being careful to keep the open end above the waterline. Hold the mold in water for 1 minute. Remove the mold from water. Press the top side of the serving platter to the open end of filled mold. Invert mold and plate in a quick motion. Aspic salad should slip effortlessly out of mold onto plate. If mold does not slip out on first try, return mold to water for 1 minute and repeat process. When aspic salad is positioned on serving platter, garnish with cilantro around base and serve.

MAKES ABOUT 6 SERVINGS.

PERSIAN POTATO-EGG SALAD

This is inexpensive but satisfying comfort food, Middle Eastern style. Unlike American potato salad, it does not require heavy mayonnaise or creamy salad dressing; instead, lemon juice and cilantro are responsible for its light, bright flavor. Served with Cream of Cilantro Soup (see page 38), it makes a wonderful summer supper.

4 large potatoes, washed well and diced with skins intact
Leaves from 1 bunch cilantro
½ cup green onions, white and green parts finely chopped
½ cup fresh lemon juice
¼ cup canola oil
1 teaspoon freshly ground black pepper
4 hard-boiled eggs, peeled and cut into round slices
Optional garnishes:
Sliced black olives
Carrot curls

Place the diced potatoes in a large pot and cover with water. Bring to boil over medium-high heat. Lower the heat to medium and cook until tender, approximately 20 minutes. Drain potatoes and let cool. Place the potatoes in a large bowl. Add the cilantro leaves, onions, lemon juice, canola oil, and pepper. Toss gently. Cover and let marinate in the refrigerator for 30 minutes. Remove the mixture from the refrigerator and portion into four serving bowls. Top with egg slices arranged in a flower or overlapping pattern, add optional garnish if desired, and serve.

MAKES 4 SERVINGS.

GARDEN SALAD WITH CILANTRO-BUTTERMILK DRESSING

You'll want to keep this delightful dressing on hand, so the recipe calls for quantities designed to make approximately 3 cups. Store the extra portion in a tightly covered jar in the refrigerator; it will keep for about a week.

Dressing:

1 cup mayonnaise

1 cup sour cream

1 cup buttermilk

1 cup chopped cilantro leaves

2 tablespoons grated Parmesan or Romano cheese

1 teaspoon dry mustard

½ teaspoon celery seeds

½ teaspoon coriander seeds

¼ teaspoon freshly ground black pepper

Place all the ingredients into a blender jar and process at high speed for one minute, or until the ingredients are very well integrated. Pour off 1 cup of the dressing into a cruet (salad dressing bottle) and set aside. Pour the remainder into a container, cover, and store in refrigerator.

MAKES ABOUT 3 CUPS.

Salad:
¼ head red cabbage
1 stalk celery
½ green bell pepper, seeded and finely chopped
1 small cucumber, peeled and finely chopped
½ cup cilantro leaves
1 tomato, cut into 8 wedges

Feed the cabbage through a food processor on the slowest speed. Turn into large bowl and reserve. Cut the celery widthwise into thin slivers. Add the celery, bell pepper, cucumber, and cilantro leaves to cabbage. Toss gently to mix. Portion salad into four serving bowls. Garnish each with 2 tomato wedges and pour about ¼ cup of the cilantro-buttermilk dressing over the top (see page 20). Serve immediately.

MAKES 4 SERVINGS.

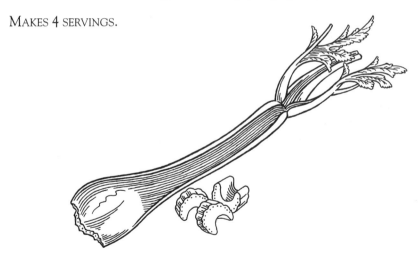

CREAMY CARROT-CILANTRO SALAD

This sprightly salad is sinfully simple to prepare, especially if you use a food processor to grate the carrots. It goes well with Cilantro-Stuffed Chicken Breasts (see page 94) or any chicken, fish, or vegetarian meal. On hot summer evenings, I serve a scoop of this salad, plus equal portions of tuna salad and Moroccan Mixed Herb Salad (see page 26) for a light dinner that requires no oven use. For a less tangy taste, substitute vanilla yogurt for lemon.

½ cup raisins
4 large carrots, grated
½ cup chopped pecan pieces
¾ cup lemon yogurt
Leaves from 1 bunch cilantro
Optional garnish:
Lettuce leaves
Wafer-thin lemon slices

Boil 1 cup of water. Place the raisins in a small bowl and cover with boiling water. Let steep for 10 minutes or until raisins begin to soften and plump. Drain off the water and reserve the raisins. Place the carrots, raisins, and pecan pieces in a large bowl. Add the yogurt and stir well. Fold in the cilantro leaves. Arrange the lettuce leaves on four small serving dishes to make a bed. Scoop the salad onto the leaves. Garnish with lemon slices and serve immediately.

MAKES ABOUT 4 SERVINGS.

TUCSON TABBOULEH SALAD

Rather than relying on overpriced packaged mixes, I encourage you to make your own *tabbuli* from scratch; the wheat will be light and slightly crunchy instead of waterlogged pulp. This recipe puts a Southwestern spin on the traditional preparation, a popular grain-and-vegetable salad originally hailing from Lebanon. Feel free to further customize the finished presentation by stirring in ¼ cup chopped fresh mint or diced black olives just prior to serving.

1 cup water
1 cup bulgur wheat
⅓ cup fresh lemon juice (do not substitute concentrated)
¼ cup olive oil
1 cup roughly chopped cilantro leaves
½ cup finely chopped green onions
2 jalapeño chili peppers, seeded, deveined, and minced
2 medium tomatoes, cut into 8 wedges each
½ large cucumber, peeled, sliced lengthwise, and cut into ¼-inch thick wedges

Combine the water and wheat in a small skillet. Bring to a boil over high heat. Immediately reduce heat to low and simmer, covered, for 5 to 6 minutes, or until the liquid is absorbed. Combine the warm cooked wheat, lemon juice, and olive oil in a large bowl, mixing well. Let cool to room temperature. Stir in the cilantro, onions, and chili peppers. Cover and refrigerate for 2 to 6 hours. Pour tabbouleh into a large serving bowl and garnish with tomatoes and cucumber wedges. Serve immediately.

MAKES 4 TO 6 SERVINGS.

MARINATED SPINACH-AVOCADO SALAD WITH HERB DRESSING

While I love cilantro's unusual flavor all by itself, I absolutely adore it when combined with just the right blend of herbs and spices, as in this lovely dressing. Though canola or any other light salad oil is recommended, a stronger, more earthy taste can be achieved by using olive oil (not extra virgin). I strongly recommend using the dark, pebbly skinned Haas avocado instead of the green, smooth-skinned Fuerte, as the latter tends to bring out cilantro's soapy flavor.

Dressing:

⅔ cup canola oil
⅔ cup chopped cilantro leaves
⅓ cup fresh lemon juice
2 tablespoons tarragon vinegar
1 teaspoon salt (optional)
½ teaspoon dried tarragon
½ teaspoon chervil
¼ teaspoon dried oregano

Place all the ingredients in a blender jar. Blend together at high speed for 30 seconds, or until thoroughly blended. Set aside.

Salad:
2 large ripe Haas avocados
½ pound fresh spinach leaves, washed well
1 cup sliced button mushrooms
½ cup cilantro leaves
Enough whole spinach leaves to line four small serving bowls

Peel, pit, and chop the avocados into ½-inch cubes. Place in large bowl and reserve. Chop the spinach leaves. Add the chopped spinach, mushrooms, cilantro leaves, and salad dressing (see page 24) to the avocado. Toss very lightly. Cover the bowl and place in refrigerator to marinate for at least 1 hour. Just before serving, arrange whole spinach leaves to line bowls. Fill bowls will marinated salad mixture and serve immediately.

Makes 4 servings.

MOROCCAN MIXED HERB SALAD

This *cooked* salad boasts a basketful of wild herbs and greens, not the least of which is cilantro! If you cannot find purslane, arugula, radicchio, or sorrel all at the same time in your supermarket, feel free to substitute watercress, dandelion greens, mustard greens, chard, or celery leaves for one or more of the ingredients listed; the taste will vary, of course, but any variety of these robust greens is a delightful detour from the usual raw romaine or spinach salad.

1 cup chopped arugula
1 cup chopped purslane
½ cup chopped radicchio
½ cup chopped sorrel
½ cup chopped watercress
1 cup chopped cilantro leaves
½ cup chopped parsley
2 cloves garlic, minced
¼ teaspoon salt
2 tablespoons canola oil
¼ teaspoon paprika
¼ teaspoon fresh lemon zest
¼ teaspoon freshly ground black pepper
1 tablespoon fresh lemon juice
Garnish:
1 tablespoon finely chopped white onion
8 green olives

Place the arugula, purslane, radicchio, sorrel, and watercress in a steamer. Steam over boiling water for 10 minutes. Place the cooked greens in a colander and let drain until cool. Press the greens gently with the back of a wooden spoon to squeeze out as much moisture as possible. Set aside and reserve. Place the cilantro leaves, parsley, garlic, and salt in a food processor. Process on high speed until the ingredients turn into a paste. Heat the oil in a medium skillet over medium-high heat. Add the cilantro paste and cook for 3 minutes, stirring constantly. Add the arugula mixture and reduce heat to medium-low. Sauté the greens for 5 minutes, or until all the liquid has evaporated, stirring constantly. Remove from heat and let cool. Add the paprika, lemon zest, and black pepper. Stir to mix well. Portion salad into four serving bowls. Sprinkle with lemon juice. Garnish each bowl with onion and 2 olives. Serve immediately.

MAKES 4 SERVINGS.

CHILLED FAJITA SALAD

Imagine the rich flavor of fajitas without frying! This clever presentation makes a hearty lunch or cold supper; the secret is to make all ingredients ahead and let chill thoroughly in the refrigerator. Serve with guacamole, sour cream, shredded cheddar, and sliced black olives for condiments.

1 red bell pepper
1 yellow bell pepper
1 green bell pepper
One 1-pound flank steak
1 cup whole cilantro leaves
¼ cup extra light olive oil
2 tablespoons red wine vinegar
2 tablespoons fresh lime juice
1 teaspoon prepared mustard
½ teaspoon salt
1 small red onion, sliced wafer thin and separated into rings
8 flour tortillas

Preheat oven to 425°F. Halve the peppers and remove the stems, seeds, and membranes. Place, cut side down, on a baking sheet. Bake for 20 minutes, or until the skins begin to blister and brown spots appear. Remove and place inside a brown paper bag. Seal bag and let peppers cool. Broil the flank steak for 20 minutes, or until it is crisped along edges and slightly pink in the middle, turning over halfway through cooking time. Remove from the oven and let cool. Slip off skins from roast-

ed peppers and cut peppers into very thin strips. Place pepper strips in a large bowl and reserve. Cut the steak into very thin slices and add to the pepper strips. Combine the cup of whole cilantro leaves, olive oil, vinegar, lime juice, mustard, and salt in a blender. Process on medium speed for 30 seconds, or until smooth. Pour the cilantro sauce over steak and pepper strips. Add the onion rings and the ¼ cup chopped cilantro leaves. Mix well. Cover the bowl and let marinate in refrigerator for at least 1 hour.

Preheat oven to 350°F. Fold each tortilla into a horn shape, securing with toothpicks. Each horn should have a tightly closed end and a wide-open mouth. Loosely ball up squares of aluminum foil and place one inside each horn (or *flauta*) so that it does not flatten. Brush the outside of each horn lightly with water. Place the *flautas* onto a nonstick baking sheet. Bake for 10 to 12 minutes, or until the tortillas are crisp and lightly browned. Remove and let cool.

Remove the fajita mixture from refrigerator and toss well. Remove the aluminum foil balls from the horns and discard (or save for next use). Stuff each horn with fajita mixture and serve with a variety of suggested condiments.

MAKES 4 SERVINGS.

SOUTHWESTERN SUMMER SALAD

My favorite Southwestern flavors combined with seasonal greens and a sweet-hot cilantro dressing . . . yum! Serve it in place of a basic lettuce-and-tomato salad for lunch or dinner, and feel free to substitute chard, sorrel, watercress, or endive for the mustard greens if you do not fancy the latter's rather peppery flavor. For a brighter dressing, combine ¼ cup salad oil, ¼ cup fresh orange juice, 2 tablespoons fresh lemon juice, 2 tablespoons minced cilantro leaves, and 1 clove of garlic, minced.

½ cup fresh lime juice
½ cup water
½ cup sugar
¼ bunch cilantro sprigs, chopped
1 jalapeño chili pepper, seeded and chopped
1 cup red leaf lettuce, shredded
½ cup butter lettuce, shredded
½ cup radicchio, shredded
½ cup cilantro leaves
½ cup mustard greens, shredded
1 large tomato, cut into 8 wedges
1 large avocado, cut into 8 slices
½ small jícama, peeled and julienned (about ½ cup)
¼ small red onion, thinly sliced and separated

Combine the lime juice, water, and sugar in a small saucepan over medium-high heat. Bring to a boil and let bubble, stirring occasionally, for 10 minutes. Add the

cilantro sprigs and chili pepper and continue boiling for 5 minutes, stirring frequently. Remove from the heat and let cool. Drain and discard the solids. Reserve the thick liquid. Toss the lettuces, radicchio, cilantro leaves, and mustard greens in a large bowl. Portion greens evenly on four plates, making a bed for other ingredients. Arrange 2 avocado slices and 2 tomato wedges on each bed of greens. Sprinkle with jícama and top with onion. Pour over the liquid dressing and serve.

MAKES 4 SERVINGS.

SOUPS

SANTA FE GAZPACHO

This sizzling variation of a classic chilled soup perfectly marries fire and ice intensities. Paired with a large serving of Cilantro Soufflé (see page 68), it makes lovely brunch or luncheon fare; it also adds a suprising amount of nutritious vegetables "invisibly" if served prior to a meat-heavy meal like Grilled Top Sirloin with Cilantro-Garlic Butter (see page 113).

4 large red tomatoes (garden style, not beefsteak)
2 large tomatillos, husks removed
2 jalapeño chili peppers, seeded and chopped (for slightly more burn, substitute serranos; for hellish heat, use 1 Habañero)
1 bunch cilantro, chopped
1 small yellow onion, diced
1 large cucumber, peeled, seeded, and diced
1 small red bell pepper, seeds and pith removed, diced
¼ cup extra light olive oil
2 tablespoons tarragon vinegar
2 tablespoons fresh lemon juice
½ teaspoon cayenne pepper
2 tablespoons mayonnaise
1 medium red tomato, seeded and finely diced
4 tablespoons finely chopped cilantro leaves
2 tablespoons finely diced green bell pepper
Garnish:
8 long shaved lemon peel curls
4 cilantro sprigs (with short stems)

Blanch the tomatoes and tomatillos in a large deep pot of boiling water for 5 minutes. Drain off the water and let the tomatoes and tomatillos cool until easy to handle. Peel off and discard the skins. Seed and chop. Place 2 red tomatoes, 1 tomatillo, 1 jalapeño, half of the cilantro bunch, and half of the chopped onion, cucumber, and red bell pepper into blender jar. Process on high speed for 1 minute, or until liquefied. Strain through fine sieve into large bowl and reserve, discarding the solids. Repeat the blending and straining process with other half of vegetables and add to original mixture. Stir in the oil, vinegar, lemon juice, cayenne, and mayonnaise.

Return the entire gazpacho base to blender jar and process on high speed for 30 seconds, or until the oil and mayonnaise are completely dispersed. Stir in the tomato, cilantro, and green bell pepper by hand. Pour gazpacho into four large serving bowls. Garnish each bowl of soup with 2 lemon curls and 1 cilantro sprig. Serve immediately for fullest flavor.

MAKES 4 LARGE SERVINGS.

CHINESE PARSLEY SOUP

This tangy, concentrated stock is bursting with flavor, so perfect for chilly winter evenings. Delicate floating cilantro leaves and crisp raw red pepper strips make a sensuous textural counterpoint to the broth, as well as adding seasonal color. Serve as the prelude to a roast fowl feast, or with a bowl of herbed brown rice and pickled vegetables for a light lunch.

1 tablespoon sesame oil
1 medium yellow onion, chopped
1 carrot, chopped
1 celery stalk, chopped
6 thin slices ginger root
1 garlic clove, chopped
5 cups water
One 6-inch piece lemon grass, cut into 1-inch sections
1 bunch cilantro
Juice of 1 lemon
1 tablespoon soy sauce
1 teaspoon cracked black peppercorns
Garnish:
4 sprigs cilantro
4 tablespoons chopped cilantro leaves
8 paper-thin slivers of raw red bell pepper

Heat the oil in a large soup pot over medium-high heat. Add the onion, carrot, celery, ginger, and garlic. Fry for 4 minutes, stirring frequently. Add the water, lemon grass, bunch of cilantro, lemon juice, soy sauce, and peppercorns. Bring to a boil, stirring occasionally. Cover pot, lower heat, and simmer for 90 minutes. Strain and pour stock into four serving bowls. Add 1 cilantro sprig, 1 tablespoon chopped cilantro leaves, and 2 slivers of red bell pepper to each bowl of broth. Serve immediately.

MAKES ABOUT 4 CUPS.

Note: The strained broth can be frozen in an airtight container; do not add garnish until just prior to serving.

CREAM OF CILANTRO SOUP

Unexpectedly refreshing, this chilled cream soup always wins raves for its robust, rich flavor.

2 cups chopped cilantro leaves
1 ¼ cups evaporated milk
1 small white onion, chopped
1 tablespoon freshly grated lemon zest
1 teaspoon freshly ground black pepper
1 cup chopped cilantro leaves
1 ½ cups chopped cilantro leaves
One 8-ounce carton plain yogurt
1 cup evaporated milk
Garnish:
Cilantro sprigs
Slivered almonds

Combine the first 2 cups of cilantro leaves, milk, onion, lemon zest, and pepper in a food processor. Process for 1 minute, or until smooth. Add 1 cup cilantro leaves. Process for 30 seconds, or until smooth. Pour into a large bowl and reserve. Combine 1 ½ cups cilantro leaves, yogurt, and 1 cup evaporated milk in food processor. Process on low speed for 30 seconds, or until nearly smooth but with some texture remaining. Pour yogurt mixture into the soup and stir gently to combine. Cover and chill for at least 1 hour. Ladle soup into serving bowls. Garnish with cilantro sprigs and slivered almonds. Serve immediately.

MAKES 4 TO 6 SERVINGS.

SIDE DISHES

CILANTRO-STUFFED BAKED TOMATOES

I love this simple side dish because it's virtually foolproof and takes very little time to prepare, letting me concentrate on the main course while it's cooking! It never fails to get appreciative comments when served alongside grilled flank steak, baked swordfish, or even Thanksgiving Day turkey!

4 medium tomatoes
Leaves from 1 bunch cilantro, finely chopped
½ cup soft bread crumbs
2 tablespoons finely shredded Gorgonzola or Romano cheese
2 tablespoons butter, melted
1 tablespoon fresh-squeezed lemon juice
¼ cup shredded Monterey Jack cheese
Garnish:
4 small cilantro sprigs

Preheat oven to 350°F. Cut a ¼-inch slice off the top of each tomato. Using a spoon, delicately scoop out the middle of each tomato. Discard pulp and seeds. Reserve the tomato shells. In a small bowl mix together the cilantro leaves, bread crumbs, Gorgonzola, melted butter, and lemon juice. Spoon the cilantro mixture evenly into tomato shells. Top each tomato with Monterey Jack cheese and place in a nonstick baking pan. Bake for 20 to 25 minutes, or until the cheese begins to bubble and turn brown in spots. Remove from the oven and serve immediately.

MAKES 4 SERVINGS.

Note: If the main course is not ready, baked tomatoes should not be left in a warm oven set on lowest setting for more than 10 minutes; tomato shells begin to get soggy and split. The tomatoes will last for 15 minutes at room temperature, if covered. Remove cooked tomatoes (for no more than a few hours), then return to a warm oven for 5 minutes before main course is ready to serve. These baked tomatoes can be frozen and reheated in a microwave.

FLUFFY ORANGE-CILANTRO RICE

Rice is a daily carbohydrate staple at my house, so I'm constantly experimenting to come up with satisfying new taste sensations. Sunflower and pumpkin seeds, and raisins and scallions combined with citrus juice are standard, but the delicate leaves of fresh coriander need special handling if their unique flavor is not to be leached by boiling water. This recipe magnificently matches any fish dish, including Pan-Seared Trout in Cornmeal (see page 88) or Dover Sole with Cilantro-Shrimp Sauce (see page 77).

2 tablespoons butter
1 small yellow onion, chopped
1½ cups water
2 tablespoons orange juice concentrate
½ teaspoon salt
1 cup brown rice
1 cup cilantro leaves, chopped

Melt the butter in a deep pot over medium-high heat. Add the onion and fry until onion becomes clear, stirring frequently. Add the water, orange juice concentrate,

and salt. Increase the heat to high and bring to a boil. Add the rice and cover pot. Lower the heat and simmer for 45 minutes, or until all water is absorbed. Remove from the heat. Gently stir in the cilantro. Re-cover the pot and let sit for 5 minutes. Fluff rice and turn into serving bowl. Serve immediately.

MAKES 4 SERVINGS.

RISOTTO WITH PORCINI MUSHROOMS AND FRESH CORIANDER

Authentic risotto is made with an extremely glutinous, very short-grained rice that is cultivated in Italy's Po River valley; one popular variety, *arborio*, is easily found in supermarkets. This side dish compliments virtually any grilled, baked, or stir-fried entrée, though it's especially fine when paired with Cilantro Soufflé (see page 68).

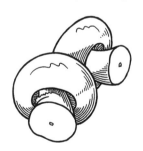

1 ounce dried porcini mushrooms
3 ¾ cups vegetable stock
2 tablespoons canola oil
1 clove garlic, sliced thin
1 ½ cups *arborio* rice
½ cup dry white wine
Juice from 1 lemon
Leaves from 1 bunch cilantro
½ cup grated dry, sharp cheese like Parmesan or Romano
4 scallions, green and white parts, chopped
¼ cup vegetable stock

Boil 1 cup of water in small pan over high heat. Add the mushrooms. Remove from the heat and cover the pan. Let the mushrooms steep for 30 minutes. Place the $3^3/4$ cups vegetable stock in a large pot and bring to boil over medium-high heat. Reduce the heat to low and let the stock simmer. Strain the mushrooms, reserving the liquid. Slice the mushrooms and reserve. Heat the oil in a large skillet over medium heat. Add the garlic and fry for 2 minutes. Add the rice and continue cooking for 1 minute, stirring constantly but very gently so as not to damage the rice kernels. Add the wine and lemon juice. Continue cooking until the liquid is absorbed, about 2 minutes, stirring constantly. Add the mushroom liquid and continue cooking until the liquid is absorbed, about 4 minutes, stirring constantly. Add 1 cup of vegetable stock, and continue cooking until the liquid is absorbed, about 6 minutes, stirring frequently, repeating the process until only three-quarters of the stock remains. Add the remaining ¾ cup vegetable stock and cook for 4 minutes, stirring frequently. Add the chopped mushrooms and cilantro leaves. Continue cooking for 2 minutes or until liquid just disappears, stirring gently. Remove from the heat. Immediately add the cheese, scallions, and ¼ cup vegetable stock. Stir quickly and serve.

MAKES ABOUT 4 CUPS.

CORIANDER HERBED TOMATOES

I first savored a version of this luscious salad as the guest of a Mexican farmer in the foothills of Baja; the secret, he said with a chuckle, was in letting the tomatoes "go one, two days too ripe." His freshly plucked, homegrown beauties luxuriated in a sunny windowsill until "the skin go soft, then into the bath they go!" While he used a basic vegetable oil "bath," the sweet-and-sour dressing used below enhances the lemony flavor of the fresh cilantro, making for a zestier dish. Serve by itself in a bowl with a loaf of crusty bread and sweet butter, or on top of a bed of butter lettuce with hard-boiled egg slices and black olives for garnish.

1 cup cilantro leaves

¼ cup extra virgin olive oil

2 tablespoons fresh-squeezed lemon juice

2 tablespoons rice wine vinegar

2 tablespoons minced chives (optional)

1 tablespoon coriander seeds

4 large very ripe tomatoes, cut crosswise into ¼-inch-thick slices

Mix together all the ingredients except the tomatoes. Arrange the tomato slices in layers in a large deep bowl, pouring some of the herbed dressing between each layer. Pour the remaining dressing over the tomatoes, tilting the bowl so all slices are covered. Cover and let marinate in refrigerator for 4 hours, occasionally spooning the marinade over top layer of tomatoes. Remove from refrigerator 15 minutes prior to serving.

MAKES 4 SERVINGS.

CILANTRO-CORN RELISH
WITH RED PEPPER

Variations of this historic Southwestern recipe can be traced along both sides of the Rio Grande, but it is believed to have first come north with the Spanish cowboys into present-day Texas sometime in the mid-1800s; put up in sterilized jars, it could last for months along a dusty trail. I love layering this relish into guacamole tacos, but it also easily accompanies barbecued beef ribs, pork, or chicken.

2 tablespoons cornstarch
⅓ cup water
2 cups freshly cut corn kernels (3 or 4 ears)
1 small red bell pepper, stemmed, seeded, and cut into very thin 1-inch strips
1 bunch cilantro, chopped
½ cup sugar
½ cup white wine or champagne vinegar
1 teaspoon coriander seeds
½ teaspoon celery seeds

Mix the cornstarch and water in a large pot over medium heat. Add the remaining ingredients. Cook for about 30 minutes, or until the mixture thickens and begins to boil, stirring frequently. Remove from the heat. Pour into an airtight container and refrigerate for at least 1 hour prior to serving. May be served cold or at room temperature. Does not freeze well.

MAKES ABOUT 2 CUPS, 4 SERVINGS.

CILANTRO SHERRIED ONIONS

Onions and fresh coriander go together like peanut butter and jelly; they're simply made for one another! Choosing sweet onions, like Bermuda or Mexican reds, is a necessity here as yellow or white varieties will overpower the delicate lemon-sage flavor of the cilantro. Beginning cooks will appreciate the easy elegance of this simple dish; serve it alongside roast beef, multigrain lentil pilaf, or brunch omelets.

⅓ **cup butter**

4 medium sweet onions, sliced into very thin rings

2 tablespoons sugar

1 teaspoon red pepper flakes

½ **cup cooking sherry**

Leaves from 1 bunch cilantro (reserve 2 sprigs for garnish)

2 tablespoons grated Asiago cheese (Parmesan or fontina can be substituted)

Melt the butter in a large saucepan over medium-low heat. Add the onions, sugar, and red pepper flakes. Cook for 5 minutes, or until barely tender, stirring frequently. Increase the heat to medium-high. Add the sherry and cilantro leaves. Cook for 5 minutes, stirring frequently. Remove from the heat to a serving dish. Sprinkle with cheese and garnish with cilantro sprigs. Serve immediately.

MAKES 4 SERVINGS.

CORIANDER POTATO BAKE

A savvy friend of mine served a simpler version of this at a dinner party recently; everyone debated as to the source of the crispy, crunchy topping. She blushingly refused to divulge her culinary secret, but nosey parker that I am, I spied the box of cornflakes on her kitchen counter and resolved to make the recipe my own. The resulting side dish goes well with meat loaf, fried chicken, or other comfort foods like grilled T-bone steak and green beans with almonds.

6 tablespoons (¾ stick) butter
4 large baking potatoes cut into thin slices
Leaves from 1 bunch cilantro
1 cup crushed cornflakes
1 cup shredded Havarti cheese (Monterey Jack may be substituted)
1 teaspoon coriander seeds
1 teaspoon black pepper

Preheat the oven to 350°F. Melt the butter in a medium casserole dish by placing in the oven for a few minutes. Spread the potatoes and cilantro leaves evenly in the dish, stirring to coat well with butter. Mix remaining ingredients in a medium bowl and sprinkle over the potato mixture. Bake for 25 to 30 minutes, or until the top is crisp and crunchy. Remove from the oven and serve immediately.

MAKES 4 TO 6 SERVINGS.

WHITE ASPARAGUS WITH CILANTRO MOCK HOLLANDAISE

Like fiddlehead ferns and ramps, white asparagus is a spring delicacy that must be prepared in season to be successful. The delicate white stalks provide a delicious contrast to the silky, pale green sauce; more robust, verdant asparagus simply won't do, darling! This aristocratic dish should be served with filet mignon, rack of lamb, roasted pheasant, or stuffed Cornish game hens.

1 pound fresh white asparagus spears
Leaves from 1 bunch cilantro, minced
¼ cup mayonnaise
¼ cup sour cream
½ teaspoon prepared mustard
1 teaspoon lemon juice

Heat the serving dish in the oven on its lowest setting. Trim off the last ½ inch of asparagus stalk ends with kitchen shears or a sharp knife. Steam the asparagus over boiling water for 8 to 10 minutes, depending on thickness of spears (spears should still be slightly crisp to the tooth when removed from heat). While the asparagus is steaming, prepare the sauce. Mix together the cilantro, mayonnaise, sour cream, mustard, and lemon juice in a food processor for 1 minute. Pour into a small saucepan and warm over low heat for 2 minutes, stirring constantly. Cover and remove the saucepan from the heat. Remove the asparagus from steamer and place on the warmed serving dish. Pour the sauce over the asparagus and serve immediately.

MAKES 4 SERVINGS.

SPICED CORIANDER CARROTS

Featuring both fresh cilantro leaves and coriander seeds, this easy-to-make side dish complements plainly prepared meat, fowl, or seafood admirably. Its sweet-and-sour undertone makes a lovely counterpoint to Barbecued T-Bone Steak with Cilantro Baste (see page 111) grilled over sweetly fragrant apple or cherry wood.

1 pound carrots, topped and peeled
2 teaspoons light brown sugar (white may be substituted)
1 clove garlic, minced
½ cup cilantro leaves
¼ cup white wine vinegar or champagne vinegar
1 tablespoon fresh lemon juice
¼ teaspoon coriander seeds
¼ teaspoon cumin
¼ teaspoon black pepper
Optional garnish:
Toasted sesame seeds

Cut the carrots into ¼-inch strips about 3 inches long. Place in a large saucepan and cover with water. Bring the water to a rolling boil over medium-high heat. Add the sugar and garlic. Boil until the carrots are just tender, approximately 6 to 7 minutes. Cover the pan and remove from the heat. Combine the remaining ingredients well in a small bowl. Drain the carrots and place in a large serving bowl. Pour the cilantro mixture over the carrots and toss well to coat. Garnish with sesame seeds and serve immediately.

MAKES ABOUT 4 SERVINGS.

CHINESE PARSLEY POTATO PANCAKES

This zesty version of a classic side dish has an unexpectedly delightful tangy twist that complements Corn-and-Coriander-Stuffed Pork Chops (see page 106), Grilled Top Sirloin with Cilantro-Garlic Butter (see page 113), and many other simply prepared chicken or meat entrées. I prefer to grate my potatoes and cilantro very finely, assuring an integrated presentation. If the pancake mixture appears too loose, add 1 tablespoon of flour; if the mixture is too dry, add 1 teaspoon of lemon juice.

4 medium potatoes
Leaves from 1 bunch cilantro
4 eggs
4 tablespoons flour
2 tablespoons fresh-squeezed lemon juice
1 teaspoon baking powder
4 tablespoons canola oil
Optional condiments:
Sour cream
Tart applesauce

Grate the potatoes and cilantro very finely using a food processor with the fine blade attachment on medium speed (or hand grate the potatoes very finely and mince the cilantro leaves). Drain any liquid and turn the mixture into a large bowl. Add the eggs, flour, lemon juice, and baking powder. Mix very well. Heat oil in medium skil-

let over medium-high heat. Drop a spoonful of the potato mixture into the hot oil and press down with the back of a spatula to make a pancake. Repeat the process until skillet is full; pancakes should not overlap. Fry the pancakes for approximately 8 minutes, or until dark golden brown, turning the pancakes over midway through the cooking time. Remove the pancakes from the skillet to a warm plate covered with paper towels. Let drain while cooking the remainder of the pancake mixture. Once all the pancakes are drained, serve immediately (with the suggested optional condiments, if so desired).

MAKES ABOUT 4 SERVINGS.

CILANTRO-STUFFED CURRIED CHAYOTE SQUASH

Chayotes are papaya-shaped, hard, light green squash that are rapidly gaining in popularity across the country for their subtle flavor. They possess an extremely large, edible seed, though some cooks discard it out of habit. This versatile vegetable can be baked, boiled, or stir-fried, just like zucchini; in this recipe we will use the seed as well as the durable shell. Ground beef or tempeh can be substituted for the turkey.

4 large chayote squash
2 tablespoons canola oil
½ medium yellow onion, finely diced
1 pound ground turkey
1 tablespoon curry powder
½ teaspoon freshly ground black pepper
2 roma tomatoes, seeded and chopped
½ cup cilantro leaves, minced
¼ cup finely diced celery stalk
8 tablespoons seasoned Italian-style bread crumbs
2 tablespoons unsalted butter, divided into 8 evenly sized pieces

Place the squash in a large pot and cover with water. Boil over medium-high heat for 25 to 30 minutes, or until the squash are just tender. Remove from the heat, drain off the water, and let cool. Split the squash lengthwise. Carefully scoop out the pulp and

seeds, leaving the shells intact. Reserve the shells. Place the pulp and seeds in a medium bowl and mash thoroughly. Set aside and reserve.

Preheat the oven to 350°F. Heat the oil in a large skillet over high heat. Add the onion and fry for 1 minute, stirring frequently. Add the turkey, curry powder, and pepper. Continue frying for 12 minutes, or until the turkey is almost completely cooked, stirring occasionally. Add the reserved squash pulp, tomato, cilantro, and celery. Continue frying for 3 minutes, or until visible liquid has evaporated, stirring frequently. Remove from the heat. Fill the reserved shells with the squash mixture. Spoon the bread crumbs over the mixture, approximately 2 tablespoons of crumbs for each shell. Place 2 pieces of divided butter on top of each stuffed shell. Place the shells in a medium baking dish and bake for 15 minutes, or until crumbs are lightly browned. Remove from oven and serve immediately.

MAKES 4 TO 8 SERVINGS.

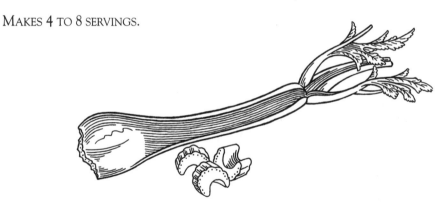

BAKED POLENTA
WITH CILANTRO CREAM

Sunny Italy meets sun-drenched Southwest in this scintillating side dish; serve it alongside Sun-Dried Tomato-Cilantro Pesto over Fusilli (see page 64), Tex-Mex Manicotti (see page 98), or any pasta dish. An older Sicilian lady of my acquaintance confided that her mother knew when the polenta was done when she could stand a spoon up in it! Indeed, when boiling the polenta, make sure it is so thick you begin to have difficulty stirring it. When making the cream, be sure not to overcook it; if it separates, stir in 1 teaspoon of fresh heavy cream at a time until texture is perfected.

1 cup yellow cornmeal
3 cups chicken stock
½ cup finely chopped sun-dried tomatoes
2 tablespoons minced cilantro leaves
½ teaspoon dried sage
4 tablespoons unsalted butter
2 eggs, lightly beaten
¼ cup grated Parmesan cheese
1 tablespoon grated Romano cheese
1 ½ cups heavy cream
⅓ cup chopped cilantro leaves
2 tablespoons minced cilantro leaves

Preheat oven to 400°F. Combine the cornmeal and stock in a large bowl, mixing well until fairly smooth with no obvious lumps. Stir in the tomatoes, 2 tablespoons minced cilantro, and sage. Pour into a large, deep pot and bring to a boil over medium-high heat, stirring very frequently. When the mixture is boiling, begin to stir constantly and cook for 10 minutes, or until the polenta is extremely thick. If the polenta begins to splatter, reduce the heat slightly and stir more vigorously. Remove from the heat and stir in the butter until it melts. Stir in the eggs and cheeses. Pour the polenta into a medium nonstick or buttered baking dish and place in the oven. Bake for 20 to 25 minutes, or until the surface is golden brown.

While the polenta is baking, make the cream. Combine the cream and chopped cilantro leaves in a small saucepan over medium heat. Bring the mixture to a boil slowly, stirring frequently. When it begins to boil, immediately reduce heat to low and let simmer for 5 to 6 minutes, or until cream mixture reduces by one-third. Remove the cream mixture from heat and strain it through a fine sieve into a heat-resistant container. Discard the cooked cilantro solids. Mix in the minced cilantro leaves and cover to keep warm. Remove the cooked polenta from the oven and slice into serving pieces. Arrange on a serving platter and drizzle with the cilantro cream. Serve immediately.

MAKES 4 TO 6 SERVINGS OF POLENTA AND APPROXIMATELY 1 CUP CILANTRO CREAM.

SPICY TWICE-BAKED SPUDS

Wonderful with Corn-and-Coriander-Stuffed Pork Chops (see page 106), Grilled Top Sirloin with Cilantro-Garlic Butter (see page 113), or any mildly spiced or non-spiced meat dish, these snazzy spuds will shake up your senses and please your palate. Do not skewer potatoes when baking or the resulting holes will allow the filling to leak out!

4 medium Idaho or other baking potatoes, scrubbed well
½ cup Gruyère cheese
¼ cup finely chopped cilantro leaves
1 jalapeño chili pepper, seeded and minced
3 tablespoons milk (for smoother potatoes, add another tablespoon milk)
2 tablespoons unsalted butter, melted
1 teaspoon cayenne powder
Hot paprika
Garnish:
Cilantro sprigs

Bake the potatoes for 45 minutes in a 400°F oven. Remove and let cool until easy to handle. Slice each potato lengthwise, removing only the top fourth of spud, making a bowl shape. Carefully scrape out most of the pulp, leaving a ¼-inch edge next to the shell. Combine the potato pulp and remaining ingredients, except for the paprika and garnish, in a large mixing bowl. Beat the potato mixture at slow speed until

fairly smooth and well combined. Spoon the potato mixture back into the skin shells, filling the shells completely and mounding mixture on top. For a more artistic presentation, use pastry bag and pipe in mixture using swirling pattern on top. Sprinkle with hot paprika. Preheat the broiler. Place the stuffed potatoes in a small nonstick or buttered baking dish. Broil approximately 6 inches from the heat for 5 minutes, or until the top of the potato mixture begins to brown. Remove from the broiler and place on a serving dish. Garnish with cilantro and serve immediately.

MAKES 4 SERVINGS.

WILD RICE FRITTERS WITH CILANTRO SOUR CREAM

While frying has fallen somewhat out of favor in the health-conscious nineties, sometimes there's just nothing as satisfying as these warm golden-brown fritters. My senses scream "Comfort food!" each time I savor their nutty, earthy flavor; paired with a tangy topping, they are an indulgence that I frequently allow myself. The recipe below does not use the traditional deep-fry method of preparation; instead, only a few tablespoons of low-fat canola oil are used to fry these fritters pancake-style, lessening my guilt and increasing my pleasure considerably.

Cilantro Sour Cream:
1 cup sour cream, warmed to room temperature
½ cup mayonnaise
¼ cup minced cilantro leaves
1 tablespoon Dijon mustard

Combine all the ingredients in a food processor. Process at low speed for 30 seconds, or until all ingredients are thoroughly combined. Spoon into bowl and cover. Reserve.

Fritters:
½ cup yellow cornmeal
½ cup whole wheat flour
2 teaspoons baking powder
½ teaspoon salt
1 cup milk
2 egg yolks
1 cup cooked brown rice (⅓ to ½ cup dried)
¼ cup cooked wild rice (⅛ cup dried)
2 egg whites
3 tablespoons canola oil

Combine the cornmeal, flour, baking powder, and salt in a large bowl and stir to mix. Combine the milk and egg yolks in a separate large bowl, beating well. Add the rice to the milk mixture and stir well to coat the grains. Pour the rice mixture into the cornmeal mixture and stir until batter is thoroughly blended. Place the egg whites in a mixer bowl and beat at medium speed for 2 minutes, or until stiff peaks begin to form. Fold the beaten egg whites into the batter. Heat the oil in a large skillet over medium-high heat. Drop spoonfuls of the batter into the oil and fry the fritters for 3 minutes, or until golden brown, turning fritters over when bubbles appear. Remove the cooked fritters with a slotted spatula to paper towels and pat dry. Keep the cooked fritters warm while frying the remaining fritters. Place a bowl of Cilantro Sour Cream in the middle of the serving platter and surround with cooked fritters. Serve immediately.

Makes 4 servings.

VEGETARIAN AND VEGAN ENTRÉES

PENNE WITH SMOKY TOMATOES AND CILANTRO

Penne is a thick and hearty shaped pasta that's wonderful for hot tossed dishes like this robust, Italian-influenced entrée. Served with hot crusty bread, a tossed green salad, and a tempting array of condiments, this simple but satisfying meal can be made in minutes. If penne is not available, ziti may be substituted; it is not recommended to use fusilli or shells.

1 pound penne
4 medium tomatoes, cut into ¼-inch-thick slices and seeded
Olive oil for brushing
2 tablespoons olive oil
2 bunches cilantro, stems and leaves roughly chopped
2 teaspoons lemon juice
Condiments:
Grated Romano or Parmesan cheese
Black olives, sliced
Raw pumpkin or sunflower seeds

Preheat the broiler. Bring 6 quarts of water to a rapid boil in a very large, deep pot. Add the penne, stirring for 30 seconds, and cook according to package directions (penne is usually boiled until it is *al dente*, approximately 12 minutes). While the penne is cooking, arrange the tomato slices on a nonstick baking sheet. Brush both sides of each slice with olive oil. Broil the tomatoes approximately 4 inches from

heat until brown spots appear on top surface, about 2 minutes. Turn the slices over and continue broiling for an additional minute (remove immediately if black spots begin to appear). Roughly chop the slices and reserve, keeping warm (cover baking sheet with foil and set aside). Heat 2 tablespoons olive oil in large skillet over medium-high heat. Add the cilantro and cook until just wilted, stirring frequently. Immediately add the lemon juice and cover the pan. Remove from the heat and reserve. When the penne is *al dente*, remove the pot from the heat and drain pasta. Place the penne in a large serving bowl. Add the chopped tomatoes and wilted cilantro sprigs. Toss gently and serve immediately with condiments.

MAKES ABOUT 4 SERVINGS.

SUN-DRIED TOMATO-CILANTRO PESTO OVER FUSILLI

I was first introduced to sun-dried tomato pesto one autumn some years ago by a friend who was catering an exquisitely tasteful Southwestern sunset wedding; riots of sun-splashed reds and golds predominated the buffet table as crimson and yellow were the bride's chosen colors. This variation pairs the rich and earthy flavor of fragrant tomatoes with the unexpected tang of lemony cilantro leaves; feel free to add more lemon juice to taste for even zestier flavor. Imported Kalamata olives are strongly recommended, but in a pinch California varieties will do.

1 pound fusilli
1 ½ cups sun-dried tomatoes (see note below)
½ cup pitted black olives
1 cup pine nuts
1 cup extra light olive oil
1 tablespoon fresh lemon juice
Leaves from 2 bunches of cilantro
Optional garnishes:
Chopped, steamed cauliflower
Sliced black olives
Crumbled feta cheese
Grated Parmesan or Romano cheese
Raw sunflower seeds
Chopped red or yellow bell pepper

Bring 6 quarts of water to boil in a large, deep pot over high heat. Add the fusilli and stir for 30 seconds, then cook according to package directions (usually until the pasta is *al dente*, approximately 12 minutes). While the pasta is cooking, place the remaining ingredients in a blender or food processor and blend them on low speed until coarsely ground (do not liquefy). If the pesto is too thick, add 1 tablespoon olive oil or lemon juice and continue processing. When the fusilli is *al dente*, drain and place in serving dish. Pour the pesto over pasta and toss gently. Serve immediately, with optional garnishes if desired.

MAKES ABOUT 4 SERVINGS.

Note: If using oil-packed sun-dried tomatoes, let drain. If using loose dried tomatoes, place in a deep bowl and cover with boiling water; let steep 10 minutes and drain prior to use.

PECOS PIZZA

Besides the ruggedly majestic beauty of the four sacred mountains, one thing that makes me frequently visit Navaho land is the freshly prepared fry bread. Whether drizzled with honey or sprinkled with powdered sugar, it is my deepest guilty pleasure. While photographing New Mexico's breathtakingly beautiful Taos pueblo, I discovered a new purpose for fry bread: Native American pizza! Variations of this hearty fare can be found as one travels south through Nambe, Santo Domingo, and Isleta pueblos into Texas; toppings can include shredded goat meat, pot cheese, sun-dried tomatoes, even corn kernels cut fresh off the locally grown cob! While fry bread is traditionally cooked in lard, my version uses the more heart-smart canola oil with little difference in flavor.

Fry Bread:
2 cups whole wheat flour
1 cup white flour
1 ½ teaspoons baking powder
½ teaspoon salt
1 ⅓ cups warm water
2 cups canola oil

Sift together the flours, baking powder, and salt into a large bowl. Add the warm water and knead the dough until soft. Remove the dough to a floured pastry board and divide into four equal-size pieces. Form each piece into a ball by hand, then flatten with your palm. Stretch and flatten the dough until it forms a round patty approximately ¼ inch thick. Heat the oil in a large skillet over high heat. Fry the

dough patties one at a time for 4 to 5 minutes, turning over once during cooking time, or until browned on both sides. Remove with tongs and place on paper towels to drain. Make the pizza.

Pizza:
4 fry breads
2 cups cooked black beans, mashed
1 cup Cilantro–Sour Cream Dip (see page 59)
2 tomatoes, seeded and chopped
2 tablespoons minced cilantro
Optional toppings:
Sliced, pitted black olives
Chopped red onion
Grated cheddar cheese
Guacamole

Arrange the fry breads on a serving platter. Spoon ½ cup of black beans on top of each bread, smearing the mash to within ½ inch of edge of bread. Spoon ¼ cup of dip on top of beans, lightly spreading it to within ½ inch of mash edge. Sprinkle each pizza with tomatoes and cilantro. Add choice of optional toppings, if desired. Serve immediately.

MAKES 4 PIZZAS.

CILANTRO SOUFFLÉ WITH CORIANDER-FETA SAUCE

Cilantro, four cheeses, and a few "insider" preparation tips make this lighter-than-air soufflé lively; it's especially recommended for those who've not yet dared to try their hand at this notoriously temperamental culinary treat.

3 ½ tablespoons unsalted butter
4 tablespoons flour
4 tablespoons minced cilantro leaves
1 ½ cups milk
2 ounces grated Gruyère cheese
2 ounces grated Gorgonzola cheese
2 ounces grated Jarlsberg cheese
2 tablespoons grated Romano cheese
½ teaspoon lemon pepper
¼ teaspoon crushed coriander seeds
6 egg yolks (room temperature)
8 egg whites (room temperature)
⅛ teaspoon salt
⅛ teaspoon cream of tartar

Preheat oven to 400°F. Butter the interior of a soufflé dish and both sides of a strip of wax paper (do not use aluminum foil; it makes for a funny taste) about 3 inches thick and long enough to go around the soufflé dish completely with ends overlapping.

Attach the "collar" to the soufflé dish by pressing the paper strip along the inside edge of the dish so that 2 inches of the collar stick up over the top. Overlap the paper ends and secure with a toothpick. Set aside.

Melt the butter in a medium saucepan over medium heat. Slowly add the flour and cilantro and cook, stirring constantly, for 3 minutes. Slowly pour in the milk and cook, whisking constantly (a spoon will not do) for 2 minutes, or until the sauce is smooth and thick. Remove from the heat. Add the cheeses, lemon pepper, and coriander seeds, stirring briskly. Allow the cheese sauce to cool to room temperature. Add the egg yolks and whisk (again, a wire whisk is vital) for 30 seconds. Reserve. Place the egg whites in a large bowl. Add the salt and cream of tartar. Whisk the egg white mixture until it is stiff and peaks begin to form (it may be very tempting to use a mixer, especially when you start breathing heavily from the exertion, but refrain). Gently fold about a fourth of the egg white mixture into the cheese mixture (this helps to keep things nice and fluffy later on). Fold the rest of the egg white mixture into the cheese mixture about 1 cup at a time. Pour the mixture—slow and easy!—into the prepared soufflé dish. Place in the oven and immediately turn down the heat to 375°F. Bake for 45 minutes, or until the top is just golden brown.

Serve with the sauce (recipe follows).

MAKES 4 TO 6 SERVINGS.

While the soufflé is baking, make the sauce as follows.

Sauce:
¾ cup heavy cream
3 tablespoons minced cilantro leaves
4 ounces crumbled feta cheese

Heat the cream and cilantro in a small saucepan over medium-high heat for 5 minutes, stirring constantly. Add the cheese 1 ounce at a time, stirring constantly, and cook for 2 to 3 minutes, or until the cheese melts and the sauce is smooth and thick. Remove from the heat and spoon onto serving portions of soufflé. Serve immediately.

MAKES 1 CUP, OR ENOUGH FOR 4 TO 6 SERVINGS OF SOUFFLÉ.

CAPPELINI PICCATA WITH CILANTRO AND CAPERS

The liberal use of fresh lemon juice (concentrate will not do) enhances the herb's own citrus topnote in this light and refreshing pasta course. Serve alongside broiled chicken breast or fish.

3 tablespoons cornstarch
¼ cup sugar
½ teaspoon salt
½ cup hot water
1 cup fresh lemon juice
2 tablespoons butter
2 teaspoons finely grated lemon zest
1 pound cappelini or angel hair pasta
1 ½ cups cilantro leaves
½ cup capers, drained, rinsed, gently patted dry
¼ cup finely diced red bell pepper

Combine the first seven ingredients in a small saucepan. Cook, stirring frequently, over medium heat for 15 to 18 minutes, or until the sauce begins to thicken. Remove from the heat and cover. The sauce will continue to thicken as it sets up. Cook the pasta according to the package directions. Rinse and drain. Place the pasta in a large bowl. Pour the lemon sauce on top and add cilantro leaves. Toss gently so that every strand is coated. Portion the pasta onto four serving plates. Sprinkle each plate of pasta with 2 tablespoons capers and 1 tablespoon red pepper. Serve immediately.

MAKES 4 SERVINGS.

GUACAMOLE TACOS WITH SALSA VERDE

These marvelous tacos are remarkable not only for their tantalizing taste but also because the shells are baked, not fried! If you prefer soft tacos that are rollable, pre-heat the oven to 400°F, place the tortillas on the middle rack, and leave for 2 to 3 minutes; you can also heat tortillas one at a time (do not stack!) by microwaving for 30 seconds, or until they begin to puff up a bit. Tip: Make up the salsa first so the guacamole doesn't brown before being used as a filling. Salsa Verde can be made a day ahead of time and refrigerated in an airtight container; some say the flavor is improved by letting the ingredients "marry" for 24 hours prior to use.

Salsa:
1 cup red wine vinegar
1 large red onion, finely diced
6 tomatillos, husked, washed well, and finely diced
1 New Mexico green chili pepper, roasted, skinned, seeded, and finely diced
1 clove garlic, finely chopped
1 tablespoon chopped parsley
1 tablespoon chopped cilantro leaves
1 teaspoon ground turmeric
1 teaspoon oregano
½ teaspoon cumin
½ teaspoon salt

Bring the vinegar to a boil in a medium saucepan. Add the onion and cook for 1 minute. Remove from the heat, add the tomatillos, and let marinate for 1 hour. Pour the tomatillo mixture into a blender jar, add the remaining ingredients, and process on low speed until thick and pulpy. Be careful not to liquefy the ingredients! Serve immediately with tacos (see recipe below), or cover and refrigerate overnight if made up ahead. Let warm to room temperature prior to serving.

MAKES ABOUT 1 ¾ CUPS, OR ENOUGH FOR 12 TACOS.

Tacos:
12 corn tortillas
6 large avocados
1 medium tomato, seeded and finely diced
2 tablespoons minced yellow onion
4 tablespoons sour cream (for extra creamy guacamole, add 2 tablespoons mayonnaise)
1 tablespoon fresh lemon juice
½ teaspoon salt
2 cups finely shredded green leaf lettuce
½ cup finely shredded radicchio
½ cup chopped cilantro leaves
1 cup shredded sharp cheddar cheese

Remove all oven racks and preheat oven to 400°F. Lightly brush one side of each corn tortilla with water. To form the tacos, drape each tortilla *dampened side facing out* over one metal rod on oven rack so that the edges hang down straight (think of hanging sheets over a laundry line). Leave an empty metal rod between each draped tortilla so tortillas will not stick together.

Place the rack on the highest level in the oven and let the tortillas bake for 3 minutes, or until the sides of the tortillas begin to crisp. Remove the taco shells from the oven and let cool.

Halve the avocados. Remove and discard pits. Scoop the pulp out of shells into a medium bowl and discard the shells. Add the tomato, onion, sour cream, lemon juice, and salt. Mash the mixture with a fork until avocado is mostly smooth, about 1 minute. Whisk the mixture for 1 minute, or until guacamole is light and fluffy with a few lumps of tomato and onion here and there. Stuff each taco shell with a layer of guacamole, topped with a layer of lettuce, then radicchio, then cilantro leaves, then cheese. Place a bowl of salsa verde with a serving spoon in the middle of a large serving platter and surround with finished tacos. Let diners drizzle as much or as little of the salsa on their own tacos as desired.

MAKES 12 TACOS, OR ENOUGH FOR 4 TO 6 SERVINGS.

FISH AND SEAFOOD ENTRÉES

DOVER SOLE WITH CILANTRO-SHRIMP SAUCE

This may be another of my secret cheater recipes for busy cooks, but the taste is purely gourmet. Peas with pearl onions, wild rice–vegetable pilaf, or Moroccan Mixed Herb Salad (see page 26) are all complementary side dishes. Cream of cauliflower soup may be substituted for cream of shrimp for a less "fishy" variation.

4 fresh Dover sole fillets, approximately ¾ pound each
2 tablespoons fresh-squeezed lemon juice
2 tablespoons butter
One 8 ¾-ounce can cream of shrimp soup
¾ cup chopped cilantro sprigs
¼ cup shredded fontina cheese (optional)

Preheat oven to 400°F. Arrange the fillets in a nonstick casserole dish. Sprinkle each fillet with lemon juice and dot with butter. Mix the remaining ingredients well in a small bowl. Pour the soup mixture over the fillets, making sure each is smothered. Place the dish in the oven and bake for 20 to 25 minutes, depending upon thickness of fillets.

MAKES 4 SERVINGS.

MONKFISH FILLETS WITH ROASTED RED PEPPER–CILANTRO SAUCE

Perk up any plain whitefish (scrod, sole) with this vibrant, chili-free salsa; pick peak-of-season peppers with deep red color and the freshest, tangiest cilantro you can find for maximum flavor impact. For a less earthy taste, remove the majority of charred skin from each pepper. I usually serve this with warm cappelini pasta tossed with sliced black olives, a bit of fresh lemon juice, and olive oil, but you can also use a mild rice pilaf as accompaniment.

3 medium red bell peppers
2 cloves garlic, chopped
1 roma tomato, seeded and chopped
2 tablespoons chopped white onion
1 tablespoon olive oil
1 tablespoon fresh lemon juice
¾ cup cilantro leaves
3 tablespoons cilantro leaves, minced
4 monkfish fillets, approximately ½ pound each
Garnish:
8 lemon slices, seeded and cut wafer thin
4 strips roasted red bell pepper
8 sprigs cilantro (just trim off ½ inch of stem's root)

Preheat oven to 500°F. Cover the bottom oven rack with aluminum foil to catch drips. Place the peppers directly on the top rack and cook for 10 minutes. Turn the peppers over and continue cooking for 10 minutes, making sure the peppers are evenly blackened (see note below). Remove the peppers and place in a heatproof bowl. Cover the bowl with foil and let the peppers steam until cool enough to handle comfortably, about 30 minutes. Remove half of each pepper's blackened skin and discard. If you remove more than half of the skin, you loose the characteristic taste, too little and the pepper has an acrid taste. Stem and seed each pepper. Cut four pepper strips approximately 3 inches long and ¼ inch wide from peeled portion of one pepper and reserve for garnish. Roughly chop peppers (not the strips) and place in blender jar. Add the garlic, tomato, onion, olive oil, lemon juice, and ¾ cup of cilantro leaves. Process on medium speed until the salsa is fairly smooth with just a hint of texture. Do not liquefy! If the salsa is too thick, add 1 teaspoon of olive oil and 1 teaspoon of water and continue processing. Add the remaining cilantro leaves and stir in by hand very gently.

Preheat the oven to 350°F. Rinse the fillets under a gentle spray of cold water. Pat dry with paper towels and set aside. Brush the inside of a nonstick casserole dish with some of the salsa. Place the fillets skin side down in the dish. Pour the remaining salsa over the fillets. Bake uncovered for about 20 minutes, or until the fish flakes easily with a fork. Remove from oven and garnish as follows: lay 1 red pepper strip in the middle of each fillet; place 1 lemon slice on either side of the pepper strip; arrange cilantro sprigs on either side of fillets. Serve immediately.

MAKES 4 SERVINGS.

Note: An alternate method for charring peppers is to place each on a spit and roast over a range's open gas flame or a barbecue grill's smoldering embers, turning frequently to ensure even blackening.

BAJA SHRIMP IN CILANTRO-WINE SAUCE

Fresh seafood and a party atmosphere can be found everywhere along the miles of golden beach that make up Baja California. During one memorable visit south of the border, my companions and I dropped in as unexpected guests on an old friend. By the time we had finished our first round of frosty margarita cocktails, our host had whipped up this under-15-minute main meal for all to enjoy! While I always recommend using seafood purchased the same day whenever possible, it's wise to keep some precleaned shrimp handy in the freezer to speed this preparation in culinary emergencies. Serve on fluffy rice or angel hair pasta.

3 tablespoons canola oil
1 clove garlic, minced
2 pounds fresh shrimp, cleaned and deveined
½ cup dry white wine
1 tablespoon fresh lemon juice
1 teaspoon fresh lemon zest
Leaves from 1 bunch cilantro

Garnish:
Sliced pimiento-stuffed green olives
Thin lemon wedges

Heat the oil in a large skillet over medium-high heat. Add the garlic and lower the heat to medium. Cook for 1 minute, stirring frequently. Add the shrimp and cook for 3 minutes, stirring occasionally. Add the wine, lemon juice, and lemon zest and cook for 4 minutes. Add cilantro leaves and continue cooking until the shrimp are white and orange, approximately 2 to 3 minutes, stirring frequently. Remove from heat and place in a serving dish. Garnish with lemon wedges and olives. Serve immediately.

MAKES ABOUT 4 SERVINGS.

BASS IN LEBANESE HOT PEPPER SAUCE

Inspired by my culinary discussions with two Lebanese brothers who operate a lovely Mediterranean-style eatery in northern Arizona, this exotic dish finds cilantro being stir-fried and then simmered! I've successfully substituted salmon steaks and red snapper for bass, and I encourage you to increase the heat intensity by adding finely chopped jalapeño or serrano chili peppers when it's time to fry the onion. Serve this entrée on a bed of brown rice pilaf with Cilantro Sherried Onions (see page 47) and Coriander Herbed Tomatoes (see page 45) on the side.

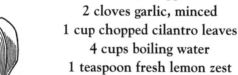

4 bass steaks, cut 1 inch thick
4 tablespoons canola oil
1 medium yellow onion, sliced and separated into rings
2 roma tomatoes, chopped and seeded
2 cloves garlic, minced
1 cup chopped cilantro leaves
4 cups boiling water
1 teaspoon fresh lemon zest
½ teaspoon cumin
½ teaspoon coriander seeds
½ cup fresh lemon juice
2 tablespoons finely chopped and pitted black olives
1 teaspoon cayenne powder
½ teaspoon freshly ground black pepper
½ teaspoon salt (optional)

Garnish:
Cilantro sprigs
Lemon wedges
Pitted black olives

Rinse the fish steaks and pat dry with a paper towel. Heat the oil in a large skillet over medium-high heat. Place the fish steaks in skillet and fry for 1 minute on each side. Remove the fish from the skillet and reserve. Add the onion, tomatoes, garlic, and cilantro leaves to skillet. Fry the onion mixture for 2 minutes, stirring constantly. Remove the skillet from the heat and carefully drain and discard the excess oil. Return the fish steaks to the skillet and arrange them over the fried onion mixture. Return the skillet to the heat. Pour enough of the boiling water over the fish steaks and onion mixture so that water comes halfway up the sides of the fish steaks. Discard remaining boiling water. Add the lemon zest, cumin, and coriander seeds. Stir gently around the fish steaks to mix in. Reduce the heat to low and simmer for 12 minutes, basting the fish steaks with sauce every 2 minutes. Remove the fish steaks to a warm serving platter. Stir in the lemon juice, chopped olives, cayenne, pepper, and salt. Remove the skillet from heat. Pour the sauce over the fish steaks. Garnish with cilantro sprigs, lemon wedges, and olives. Serve immediately.

MAKES ABOUT 4 SERVINGS.

GRILLED MARLIN WITH CILANTRO-CITRUS COMPOTE

The tartness of the cilantro marinade that flavors this delicious fish is reinforced by a vibrant compote that will have your taste buds sizzling! Serve it alongside Cilantro Sherried Onions (see page 47) and wild rice pilaf.

Note: While this recipe calls for the fish to be grilled, it can also be barbecued outside over wood chips or charcoal, or broiled.

1 cup chopped cilantro leaves
¼ cup olive oil
1 clove garlic, chopped
3 tablespoons grated Parmesan cheese
1 tablespoon grated pecorino Romano cheese
2 tablespoons chopped walnuts
½ teaspoon grated lime peel
¼ cup fresh lime juice
¼ cup olive oil
4 marlin steaks ¾ to 1 inch thick, about ⅓ pound each
(swordfish may be substituted)

For the compote:
4 grapefruit sections, membranes and seeds removed
¼ cup minced cilantro leaves
1 jalapeño chili pepper, seeded, deveined, and minced
1 clove garlic, minced
1 tablespoon fresh lime juice
2 teaspoons olive oil

Combine the first seven ingredients in a food processor running on medium speed. Process until the mixture has a pastelike texture. Add the lime juice and olive oil. Process on slow speed until the mixture has thinned but still possesses some texture. Reserve. Arrange the marlin steaks in a medium baking dish and pour the marinade over. Turn the steaks so that the flesh is covered evenly with marinade. Cover the dish and refrigerate for 3 hours, turning the steaks over every hour. Preheat grill using the medium-heat setting. Pour off the marinade and discard. Place the marinated steaks on a rack and grill for 5 minutes. While the fish is cooking, prepare the compote as follows.

Dice the grapefruit sections into ¼-inch pieces. Place in a small bowl. Add the cilantro leaves, chili pepper, garlic, lime juice, and olive oil. Stir well to combine and reserve.

Turn the steaks over and continue grilling the fish for an additional 5 minutes. Transfer the steaks to a serving platter and top each with the compote. Serve immediately.

MAKES 4 SERVINGS.

EL PASO PESTO WITH LINGUINE, CAVIAR, AND CHEVRE

Go beyond basic basil and pine nuts with this snappy Southwestern take on traditional pesto. While I've created various versions of cilantro pesto, I think this upscale treatment (fueled by chili pepper firepower) is my all-time favorite; and while I usually prefer black caviar, the contrast of red roe, white goat cheese, and vibrantly green pasta is irresistible. These are, coincidentally, the colors of the Mexican flag, making this dish perfect for urban Cinco de Mayo celebrations.

1 pound linguine
2 cups chopped cilantro leaves
1 cup chopped parsley leaves
2 jalapeño chili peppers, skinned, seeded, and chopped
¼ cup toasted almond slivers
½ cup light olive oil
¼ cup grated Parmesan cheese
2 tablespoons grated Romano cheese
1 teaspoon fresh lemon juice
¼ teaspoon cayenne pepper
1 cup cilantro leaves
8 ounces chevre goat cheese, cut into 8 thin slices, covered and refrigerated
4 teaspoons red salmon roe

Cook the pasta according to package directions. Meanwhile, combine the chopped cilantro leaves, parsley leaves, jalapeño, almond slivers, olive oil, Parmesan and Romano cheeses, lemon juice, and cayenne pepper in a food processor. Process at low speed for 30 to 60 seconds, or until a thick paste has formed (be careful not to liquefy!). Set aside and reserve. Remove the goat cheese from refrigerator just before the pasta is done. Drain the cooked pasta, rinse, and place in a large bowl. Add the reserved pesto and 1 cup cilantro leaves and toss, making sure every strand is coated. Portion the linguine onto four serving plates. Top each pile of pasta with 2 slices of chevre and 1 teaspoon of roe. Serve immediately.

MAKES 4 SERVINGS.

PAN-SEARED TROUT IN CORNMEAL WITH CILANTRO-LEMON BUTTER

Running through the middle of Sedona, Arizona, beautiful Oak Creek provides an abundance of plump 10-to-12-inch trout in every season. This recipe is a local favorite; for more of the Southwest's spicy flavor, add ½ tablespoon crushed red pepper flakes or cayenne pepper to the cornmeal mix prior to cooking. Serve with Wild Rice Fritters with Cilantro Sour Cream (see page 59) or Risotto with Porcini Mushrooms and Fresh Coriander (see page 43).

Butter:
¾ cup (1 ½ sticks) unsalted butter, softened
¼ cup minced cilantro leaves
Juice of ½ lemon
½ teaspoon salt
½ teaspoon finely grated lemon zest
¼ teaspoon white pepper

Combine all the ingredients in a food processor. Process at low speed for 1 minute, or until the butter mixture is fairly smooth and slightly fluffy. Use a mini-scooper to scoop out 8 butter balls. Place the balls on a plate, cover, and refrigerate. Spoon remaining butter mixture into a small pan. Melt over low heat. Cover and keep warm over very low heat while making fish.

Fish:
4 brown, rainbow, or other 10-to-12-inch plump trout
½ cup yellow or blue cornmeal
1 ½ tablespoons white or whole wheat flour
1 tablespoon minced cilantro leaves
⅛ teaspoon salt
⅛ teaspoon white pepper
⅓ cup milk
2 tablespoons melted lemon-butter mixture (see page 88)
Garnish:
Lemon wedges
Cilantro sprigs

Split the trout lengthwise and clean, removing the head but leaving the tail and skin intact. Combine the cornmeal, flour, cilantro, salt, and pepper in a shallow casserole dish. Using a paper towel, swab the trout flesh with milk. Immediately press the coated flesh into the cornmeal mixture to cover. Place trout, coated side up, on flat surface and allow to dry for 20 to 25 minutes.

Heat the melted butter mixture in a large skillet over medium-high heat. Fry the trout individually for 5 minutes on each side, adding additional melted butter mixture if necessary so the pan doesn't dry out. Remove each cooked trout from the pan. Pat the cornmeal side dry with a paper towel and keep warm while cooking the remaining fish. Arrange all the cooked trout on serving platter with lemon wedges and cilantro sprigs. Top each fish with 2 refrigerated butter balls and serve immediately with excess melted lemon-butter in a small sauceboat.

MAKES 4 SERVINGS.

FOWL ENTRÉES

CHINESE PARSLEY CHICKEN WITH CILANTRO-PINEAPPLE SAUCE

Answer the call of the tropics with this sweet mealtime treat; cilantro's lemon-sage flavor changes perceptibly when paired with pineapple, bringing out its herbal wholesomeness. Serve this broiled chicken main course with Fluffy Orange-Cilantro Rice (see page 42) and Spiced Coriander Carrots (see page 50).

Pineapple sauce:
½ cup (1 stick) butter
1 teaspoon cornstarch
½ cup cilantro leaves, finely chopped
⅓ cup pineapple syrup from 10 ¾-ounce can (reserve pineapple rings)
¼ cup fresh-squeezed lemon juice
1 teaspoon soy sauce

Melt the butter in a medium pot over medium-high heat. Stir in the cornstarch. Add the remaining ingredients and bring to a boil, stirring constantly. Lower the heat and simmer for 5 minutes, stirring constantly. Cover and remove from the heat. Use on chicken as directed below.

Chicken:
4 tablespoons (½ stick) butter, melted
Two 2-pound broiling chickens, cut into serving pieces
Pineapple sauce (see above)
8 pineapple rings from 10 ¾-ounce can (reserved from sauce recipe)
8 maraschino cherries

Optional garnish:
Cilantro sprigs
Cashew pieces
Wafer-thin lemon slices

Preheat the broiler. Brush half the melted butter on chicken pieces and arrange on the broiler pan skin side down. Broil 6 inches from heat for 20 minutes, or until the pieces are lightly browned. Remove the pan from the broiler. Turn the chicken pieces and baste with the remaining melted butter. Return the pan to the broiler and continue broiling for 15 minutes. Remove the pan from the broiler. Add the pineapple rings around the chicken. Place a cherry in the middle of each pineapple ring. Brush the cherries and tops of the pineapple rings with pineapple sauce. Baste both sides of chicken pieces with pineapple sauce. Pour any remaining sauce over the chicken pieces and return the pan to the broiler. Broil for 5 minutes, or until pineapple starts to turn golden brown. Remove from the broiler. Sprinkle optional garnish over the chicken, if desired. Serve immediately.

MAKES 4 TO 6 SERVINGS.

CILANTRO-STUFFED CHICKEN BREASTS

This elegant-looking entrée is a snap to prepare, but it tastes as if you've slaved all day over a hot stove! Serve it with a simple lentil-rice pilaf, couscous, or Wild Rice Fritters with Cilantro Sour Cream (see page 59) when you want to reward yourself.

3 large skinless, boneless, whole chicken breasts
3 ounces cream cheese, softened
½ cup cilantro leaves, finely chopped
¼ cup finely chopped button mushrooms
2 tablespoons finely chopped pitted black olives
1 egg
1 tablespoon water
3 tablespoons white flour
2 cups bread crumbs
Garnish:
Cilantro sprigs
Pitted black olives

Preheat oven to 350°F. Place the chicken breasts between plastic wrap layers and pound with a mallet until ¼ inch thick. Set aside. Beat together the cream cheese, cilantro, mushrooms, and olives on low speed for 30 seconds, or until well mixed. Spread one side of each chicken breast with the cream cheese mixture. Fold in half (see note) so that the mixture is inside the chicken breast and secure with toothpicks. Set aside. Beat together the egg and water on medium speed for 10 seconds. Set aside.

Dredge both sides of the stuffed chicken breasts in flour, then egg wash, then bread crumbs. Make sure each piece is thoroughly coated. Place the coated breasts in a medium buttered baking dish and bake for about 50 minutes, or until the chicken is thoroughly cooked. Remove from the oven and slice each breast in half. Arrange the pieces on a warm serving platter and garnish with cilantro sprigs and olives. Serve immediately.

MAKES ABOUT 4 SERVINGS.

ANCHO CHILI CHICKEN STEW

This modern Southwestern recipe can trace its heritage back to the *pipians*, or stews, of nineteenth-century Mexico. While pumpkin seeds are traditionally found at the heart of such stews, in truth almonds, peanuts, walnuts, or even sesame seeds can be used to thicken the sauce. Since this recipe calls for an added measure of cilantro, I've used peanuts for a bold matchup of flavors. Serve this entrée with Cilantro-Stuffed Curried Chayote Squash (see page 53) and Spanish rice.

One 3-pound chicken, cut into serving pieces
1 medium yellow onion, chopped
½ bunch cilantro (reserve other half, see below)
1 carrot, chopped
1 celery stalk, chopped
2 cups chicken stock
6 ancho chili peppers, seeded and finely chopped
2 cups boiling water
½ cup roasted unsalted peanuts
2 tablespoons canola oil
¼ teaspoon ground cinnamon
¼ teaspoon ground cloves
¼ teaspoon salt
⅛ teaspoon coriander seeds
⅛ teaspoon ground nutmeg
Leaves from ½ bunch cilantro (see above)

Place the chicken, onion, cilantro sprigs, carrot, celery, and chicken stock in a large, deep skillet. Bring the liquid to a boil over high heat. Cover the skillet. Reduce heat to low and simmer for 45 minutes, turning the chicken pieces over halfway through cooking time. While the chicken is cooking, place the chili peppers in a small bowl and cover with boiling water. Let steep for 45 minutes, stirring occasionally. Remove the skillet from heat and uncover. Remove the chicken from the skillet. Drain off and reserve the stock from the skillet. Return the chicken to the skillet and cover to keep warm.

Place the soaked chilis in a food processor. Add the peanuts and process for 2 minutes on high speed, or until a thick paste is formed. Heat the oil in a second large skillet over medium-high heat. Add the chili mixture, cinnamon, cloves, salt, coriander seeds, and nutmeg. Fry for 3 minutes, stirring constantly. If the mixture is too dry, add 2 tablespoons of the reserved stock. Slowly add 2 cups of the reserved stock. Continue cooking for 3 minutes, stirring frequently. Reduce the heat to low. Add the chicken pieces and continue cooking for 5 minutes, stirring occasionally. Remove chicken pieces to serving platter and cover with sauce. Sprinkle the cilantro leaves over the chicken and serve immediately.

MAKES ABOUT 4 SERVINGS.

TEX-MEX MANICOTTI

Savory stuffed pasta shells are smothered in salsa; perfect for Sunday brunch! Start with Santa Fe Gazpacho (see page 35) or Southwestern Summer Salad (see page 30), and finish off the meal with summery Cilantro-Citrus Fluff with Mango and Papaya (see page 133).

2 skinless, boneless chicken breast halves

½ teaspoon freshly ground black pepper

2 large tomatoes, seeded and diced into ½-inch cubes

2 serrano chilis, seeded and minced

½ medium red onion, diced into ¼-inch cubes

½ cup cilantro leaves, chopped

2 cloves garlic, minced

½ tablespoon tarragon vinegar (or red wine vinegar)

1 teaspoon olive oil

8 manicotti shells

1 cup ricotta cheese

2 scallions, finely chopped

¼ cup pitted, sliced black olives

¼ cup cilantro leaves, minced

Preheat the broiler. Arrange the chicken breast halves on a flat baking sheet. Sprinkle with pepper and broil for 15 minutes, or until just cooked, turning breasts over halfway through cooking time. Remove from the broiler and let cool. Combine the tomatoes, chilis, red onion, chopped cilantro leaves, garlic, vinegar, and olive oil

in a large bowl. Set the salsa aside and reserve. Boil the manicotti shells according to package directions.

Preheat oven to 350°F. Dice the broiled chicken breasts and place in medium bowl. Add the cheese, scallions, olives, and minced cilantro leaves to the chicken and mix well. Drain the manicotti shells and stuff with the chicken mixture. Arrange the manicotti in a medium nonstick or buttered baking dish. Smother with salsa and place in oven. Bake for 15 minutes. Remove from the oven and serve immediately.

MAKES 4 SERVINGS.

CHICKEN WITH MOLE VERDE SAUCE

Mole is the Mexican word for stew, though most gringos think only of the complicated chocolate-based sauce when they hear the word. This particular mole is one of my favorites because it's such a cinch to prepare, yet possesses a uniquely spirited flavor. Served to me in Angel Fire, New Mexico, with piping-hot buttered corn tortillas for dipping and a big bowl of fluffy rice, it immediately banished all snowbound winter blues.

2 tablespoons canola oil
One 3-pound chicken, cut into serving pieces
2 cups chicken stock
1 large onion, diced
2 cloves garlic, chopped
1 ½ cups cilantro leaves, chopped
½ cup parsley sprigs, chopped
2 leaves romaine lettuce, chopped
3 serrano chili peppers, seeded and chopped
½ cup plus 2 tablespoons diced almonds
2 tablespoons canola oil

Heat the first 2 tablespoons of canola oil in a large skillet over medium-high heat. Add the chicken and cook for 5 minutes, or until lightly browned. Add the stock. Increase the heat to high and bring the stock to a boil. Reduce the heat to low and cover the skillet. Simmer the chicken for 45 minutes, or until tender. While the chicken is cooking, place the onion, garlic, cilantro, parsley, lettuce, serranos, and almonds in a food processor. Process until the mixture is a thick paste. Reserve the paste. Remove the skillet from the heat. Remove the chicken pieces and reserve. Drain off the stock and reserve. Heat the canola oil in the same skillet over medium heat. Add the paste and cook for 3 minutes, stirring constantly. Add the reserved stock and cook for 3 minutes, stirring frequently. Reduce heat to low. Add reserved chicken pieces and cook for 10 minutes, stirring frequently and turning the chicken over halfway through the cooking time. Remove the chicken to a serving dish. Pour the sauce over the chicken and serve immediately.

MAKES ABOUT 4 SERVINGS.

BAKED CHICKEN WITH SHALLOT-CILANTRO SAUCE PIQUANTE

A friend, freshly returned from island-hopping in sunny Caribbean climes, brought me a beautiful description of his latest culinary find; this recipe re-creates the piquant palate pleaser for all to enjoy. Serve island-style with white rice and hot grilled mango slices plus green or white asparagus spears.

1 cup finely chopped shallots
½ cup boiling water
¼ cup finely chopped cilantro leaves
¼ cup minced chives
2 cloves garlic, minced
2 serrano chili peppers, seeded and minced
3 tablespoons fresh lime juice
1 tablespoon honey
1 tablespoon orange marmalade
½ teaspoon freshly ground black pepper
½ teaspoon salt (optional)
One 3-pound chicken, cut into serving pieces
Garnish:
Lime wedges
Cilantro sprigs

Mix all ingredients except for the chicken in a medium bowl. Cover and let stand at

room temperature for 1 hour. Preheat oven to 350°F. Arrange the chicken in a baking dish. Uncover the sauce and stir twice. Pour the sauce over the chicken, making sure each piece is evenly covered. Place the chicken in the oven and bake for 40 to 45 minutes, turning the pieces over halfway through the cooking time and basting with the sauce. Remove from the oven and garnish with lime wedges and cilantro sprigs. Serve immediately.

MAKES ABOUT 4 SERVINGS.

MEAT ENTRÉES

LAMB CHOPS WITH CILANTRO-PARMESAN SPREAD

Slow-cooked rack of lamb is renowned for its flavorful herb crust; now you can get the same mouth-watering goodness in mere minutes. Topped with the unexpectedly delightful flavor of cilantro, juicy broiled chops should be served with Spicy Twice-Baked Spuds (see page 57) and Cilantro Sherried Onions (see page 47) for an elegant evening repast.

8 lamb chops, about 1 inch thick
Leaves from 1 bunch cilantro, minced
¼ cup grated Parmesan cheese
4 tablespoons butter, softened

Preheat the broiler. Arrange the lamb chops on a broiler pan. Place the pan in the broiler so that the chops are 3 inches from the heat. Broil chops for 5 to 8 minutes, or until lightly browned. While the chops are cooking, combine the remaining ingredients in a small bowl, mashing well to make a thick paste (think pesto consistency). Remove the chops from the broiler and turn. Return to broiler for 4 minutes. Remove the chops from the broiler and spread the cilantro mixture on the top side of the meat. Return the chops to the broiler and cook for 1 minute, or until the cheese begins to brown. Remove from broiler and serve immediately.

MAKES 4 SERVINGS.

CORN-AND-CORIANDER-STUFFED PORK CHOPS

Your family will think you've slaved for days over this deceptively easy to make dish; a hint of sage brings out the herbal side of cilantro's unique flavor. Serve with Risottto with Porcini Mushrooms and Fresh Coriander (see page 43) or a medley of fresh steamed vegetables like chayote and summer squash with cauliflower.

4 double-thick pork chops
½ cup corn kernels cut from cob
½ cup cilantro leaves, chopped
⅓ cup soft bread crumbs
1 tablespoon fresh orange zest
¼ teaspoon sage

Cut a pocket between the first and second rib of each chop starting at the round end and working in to ½ inch away from the bone edge. Set aside. Mix the remaining ingredients well in a small bowl. Fill the chop pockets with the stuffing mix. Seal the pockets by inserting toothpicks at an angle into the round edge of the chops. Arrange the stuffed chops in a large skillet. Cook for 10 minutes over medium-high heat, or until the bottom side is just lightly browned. Turn the chops over and repeat the process. Lower the heat to simmer and add ½ cup hot water. Cover the skillet and cook for 35 to 40 minutes, or until the chops are no longer pink inside. Add more water if necessary to keep the liquid level constant. Remove the chops from the skillet. Remove the toothpicks from the chops and serve immediately.

MAKES 4 SERVINGS.

ROAST PORK WITH GREEN MANGO CILANTRO RELISH

For the most authentic tropical flavor, select mangoes that are firm (not rock hard), green-skinned, and almost ripe; the flesh inside should be light yellow to pale gold and tart tasting. If the flesh gives when squeezed, the fruit will be very sweet and orange in color—delicious, but not suitable for this recipe.

Relish:
2 green, almost ripe mangoes
Leaves from ½ bunch of cilantro
(reserve other half of bunch for roast; see below)
1 tablespoon sesame oil
1 tablespoon fresh lime juice
1 tablespoon minced red bell pepper, seeded
1 tablespoon minced jalapeño chili pepper, seeded
1 tablespoon freshly grated lime zest
1 teaspoon minced garlic

Peel the mangoes and cut the flesh from the seeds. Discard the seeds. Chop the mango flesh into ½-inch cubes. Place the chopped mango in a medium bowl. Roughly chop the cilantro leaves. Add the chopped leaves and remaining ingredients to the mango. Toss gently. Cover and refrigerate until the roast is cooked. Just before the roast is ready to be removed from the oven, remove the relish from the refrigerator. Let the relish warm to room temperature prior to serving.

Roast:
One 3-pound pork roast, closely trimmed
¼ cup fresh lemon juice
¼ cup fresh lime juice
2 bay leaves, crushed
½ bunch cilantro, chopped
2 tablespoons minced garlic
1 tablespoon canola oil
1 teaspoon freshly ground black pepper
½ teaspoon ground cumin
½ teaspoon crushed coriander seeds

Shallowly pierce the roast all over. Place in a deep bowl. In a small bowl, mix the remaining ingredients well. Pour the mixture over the roast. Turn the roast so that its surface is evenly coated. Cover the bowl and let the roast marinate for 1 hour at room temperature, turning every 15 minutes, or place in refrigerator for at least 3 hours, turning every 30 minutes.

Preheat oven to 350°F. Remove the meat from bowl and place in a roasting pan. Pour ¼ cup of the marinade into the bottom of the roasting pan. Reserve the remaining marinade for basting. Place the meat in the oven and bake for 2 to 2 ½ hours, or until the meat is well browned and thoroughly cooked. While the meat is baking, baste with the reserved marinade and turn the roast over every 30 minutes. Remove from the oven and let cool for 10 minutes. Cut the meat into thick slices. Arrange the slices on a large platter around a bowl of green mango–cilantro relish (see page 107). Serve immediately.

MAKES ABOUT 4 SERVINGS.

VEAL IN PIPIAN SAUCE

While I am not a veal fan, any cookbook focusing on cilantro-dominated recipes would be remiss if it did not include this classic Mexican entrée. This particular pipian, or stew, arrived via my mailman's wife (of the Mescalero Apache tribe) and obtains its lush green hue from pumpkin seeds, cilantro, tomatillos (green husk tomatoes), and romaine lettuce; serve it with warmly colored Spiced Coriander Carrots (see page 50) or baked tomatoes and white rice for a dazzling color contrast.

3 pounds boneless veal shank, cut into 1-inch and 2-inch pieces
2 cups chicken stock
1 cup raw pumpkin seeds
One 12-ounce can of tomatillos, or 6 fresh tomatillos with husks removed, chopped
1 cup cilantro leaves, chopped
2 romaine lettuce leaves, chopped
1 large yellow onion, chopped
1 New Mexican green chili pepper, seeded and chopped
1 jalapeño chili pepper, seeded and chopped
1 clove garlic, chopped
2 tablespoons canola oil
1 teaspoon freshly ground black pepper
¼ cup cilantro leaves, finely chopped

Place the veal in a large skillet and cover with stock. Simmer over low heat for 1 hour, or until the meat is tender, stirring occasionally. Remove the skillet from the

heat, cover, and reserve. Place the pumpkin seeds in an ungreased large skillet and lightly toast over medium-high heat for 3 minutes, shaking the skillet vigorously to keep the seeds from burning. Remove the skillet from the heat and let cool for 5 minutes. Place the toasted seeds in a food processor and grind on high speed for 2 minutes. Add the tomatillos, cilantro leaves, and lettuce leaves. Process on medium speed for 1 minute. Add the onion, chili peppers, and garlic. Process on medium speed for 2 minutes, or until mixture becomes a thick paste. Heat the oil in an ungreased large skillet over medium-high heat. Add the paste and fry for 2 minutes, stirring constantly; if mixture is too dry, immediately add 2 tablespoons of chicken stock taken from the veal. Drain off the chicken stock from the veal and add to the pipian paste. Add the black pepper and stir well. Add the veal to the pipian sauce. Reduce the heat to the lowest setting and simmer for 2 minutes, stirring occasionally. Remove the veal and sauce to the serving dish. Sprinkle with finely chopped cilantro leaves and serve immediately.

MAKES ABOUT 4 SERVINGS.

BARBECUED T-BONE STEAK WITH CILANTRO BASTE

For a lighter, more sweet undertone, grill the meat over apple or cherry wood instead of mesquite coals; the difference is delicious! The combination of herbs and pepper permeate the beef through a lengthy marination process; the flavor is reinforced by using the marinade as a baste during grilling. Serve this entrée with heaping bowls of Salsa Fresca (see page 10), Cilantro–Sour Cream Dip (see page 12), corn chips, and crudités. Crudités are a snappy assortment of raw vegetables including carrot, celery, zucchini, and jícama sticks; red radishes; cauliflower and broccoli florets; and cucumber slices. The taste variations are endless.

1 cup cilantro leaves, chopped
½ cup extra light olive oil
½ cup walnut oil (canola can be substituted)
½ cup red wine vinegar
½ cup fresh lemon juice
4 cloves garlic, chopped
2 teaspoons cayenne pepper
1 teaspoon oregano
1 teaspoon salt
1 teaspoon freshly ground black pepper
4 T-bone steaks, 12 to 14 ounces each

Mix all the ingredients except the steaks in a large bowl. Place 2 steaks in each of 2 large plastic bags with zippered locks. Pour half of the marinade into each bag and seal tightly. Turn the bags to coat the meat evenly. Place the bags in the refrigerator and marinate overnight, or let marinate at room temperature for 2 hours, turning the bags frequently. When the coals are ready, remove the steaks from the bags and place on the grill. Pour the marinade out of the bags into a medium bowl. Baste the steaks frequently with marinade during the grilling process. The grilling time will vary, depending on the grill, but cook for about 10 to 12 minutes for rare, 12 to 14 minutes for medium, and 14 or more minutes for well done. Place the cooked steaks on serving platters and serve immediately. Discard any leftover marinade. If you prepare this in a broiler, subtract about 2 minutes from the cooking times.

MAKES 4 SERVINGS.

MARINATED AND GRILLED TOP SIRLOIN WITH CILANTRO-GARLIC BUTTER

Cilantro and garlic flavor themes reinforce the delectable smoky taste of juicy grilled steaks through a spicy marinade and a scrumptious cilantro-garlic butter baste. Serve the finished steaks with Wild Rice Fritters with Cilantro Sour Cream (see page 59) or Spicy Twice-Baked Spuds (see page 57), plus fresh steamed vegetables. When handling Habanero chilies, wear rubber or plastic gloves; wash hands immediately after contact with any chili pepper.

Marinade:

2 cups tomato juice

½ cup olive oil

2 bunches cilantro, chopped

12 cloves garlic, chopped

1 small Habañero chili pepper, seeded, deveined, and finely chopped (or 6 jalapeño chili peppers, finely chopped, for less spicy heat)

4 top sirloin steaks, 14 to 16 ounces each

Place all the ingredients except the steaks in a large saucepan over medium-high heat. Bring the mixture to a boil. Immediately lower the heat and let simmer for 10 minutes. Remove the marinade from the heat and let cool to room temperature. Arrange the steaks in a large casserole dish so that the sides are not overlapping. Pour the marinade over the meat. Turn the steaks once to make sure all sides are evenly coated. Cover and refrigerate for 12 to 24 hours, turning the meat every 4 to 6 hours (except when sleeping, of course). Just before grilling, make the butter.

Butter:
1 ½ cups (3 sticks) unsalted butter, softened
4 tablespoons minced cilantro leaves
3 cloves garlic, minced
1 teaspoon minced chives
⅛ teaspoon dry mustard

Place all the ingredients in a food processor. Process at low speed for 30 to 45 seconds, or until all ingredients are thoroughly combined and the butter is just whipped. Remove to a small bowl.

Remove the meat and discard the marinade. Use a mini-scoop to form 8 small butter balls. Place the balls on a small plate, cover with plastic wrap, and refrigerate. Spoon the remaining butter into a small saucepan and melt over low heat. Pour the butter into a small bowl and use as a baste. When the coals are ready, place the marinated steaks on the grill and baste their top sides with melted butter. Turn the steaks frequently during the cooking process and brush on the baste liberally. Grill steaks for 15 to 20 minutes, or until desired degree of doneness, making sure to use up all of the melted butter. Remove the steaks from the grill and arrange on a serving platter. Top each steak with 2 refrigerated butter balls and serve immediately. If you prepare this in a broiler, subtract about 2 minutes from the grilling time.

MAKES 4 STEAKS.

EXTRAS

CHINESE PARSLEY FAN BISCUITS

While I normally don't recommend using prepackaged items in my recipes, this little cheater is so scrumptious that I can't resist passing it on. A bachelor buddy of mine used this steaming bread basket to warm up a special lady he invited over for dinner. "She couldn't believe that I worked so hard all day, then turned out something so artistic and savory for her," he enthused. "It really made a great first impression." Do I need to mention that this couple is now engaged?

2 tablespoons butter
1 teaspoon fresh-squeezed lemon juice
4 tablespoons finely chopped cilantro leaves
1 teaspoon red pepper flakes
8 brown-and-serve-style butterflake refrigerator rolls

Melt the butter in a small saucepan over low heat. Stir in the lemon juice, cilantro leaves, and red pepper flakes. Remove from the heat and reserve. Arrange the rolls in a baking pan. Gently separate the sections on top of each roll. Brush the butter-cilantro mixture into the crease between each section. Brush the remaining mixture onto the tops of the rolls. Bake according to package directions (approximately 350°F for 10 to 12 minutes) and serve while steaming.

MAKES 8 ROLLS.

GRIDDLED CRAB-CILANTRO FINGER SANDWICHES

Boffo for buffet, these hearty little sandwiches can be kept warm in a chafing dish or on a griddle turned to its lowest setting. Arranged on a platter and served with summer fruit salad, they make a wonderful, easily handled main course for children's parties. *Surimi* (whitefish) can be substituted for crabmeat for a milder seafood flavor.

1 cup cooked crabmeat, drained and flaked
Leaves from 1 bunch cilantro, chopped
⅓ cup mayonnaise
¼ cup finely diced celery stalk
1 tablespoon fresh-squeezed lemon juice
12 slices sourdough bread, crusts trimmed
½ cup (1 stick) butter, melted
Garnish:
36 small cilantro sprigs
18 pimiento-stuffed green olives, sliced in half widthwise

Preheat the griddle. Mix the crabmeat, cilantro leaves, mayonnaise, celery, and lemon juice together in a food processor on low speed until fairly smooth. Set aside and reserve. Cut each slice of bread into three equal-size strips. Brush one side of each slice of bread with melted butter. Spread the crab mixture onto the unbuttered side of each slice of bread. Place each sandwich buttered side down onto the hot griddle. Cook until the bread is golden brown, about 3 to 5 minutes. Remove to a serving tray. Garnish each sandwich with a small cilantro sprig and sliced green olive. Serve immediately.

MAKES 36 FINGER-SIZE, OPEN-FACE SANDWICHES, OR ENOUGH TO SERVE 6 TO 8 PEOPLE.

COCONUT-CORIANDER CHUTNEY

Some friends who own an East Indian eatery in Flagstaff, Arizona, simply delight in surprising me with unusual flavor combinations; from tangy sauerkraut curry to scorching chili pepper–stuffed bread, their Delhi heritage never ceases to amaze me, especially expressed as it is in the middle of cowboy country! But this lip-smackin' and very versatile chutney of mine gained me some brownie points with the restaurateurs; they now use it as a dip, smother baked fish with it, and lavish it into *biryani*, a vegetable casserole. You can use it to accompany broiled chicken breasts, too.

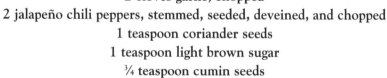

1 cup cilantro leaves
½ cup unsweetened grated coconut
¼ cup fresh-squeezed lemon juice
2 cloves garlic, chopped
2 jalapeño chili peppers, stemmed, seeded, deveined, and chopped
1 teaspoon coriander seeds
1 teaspoon light brown sugar
¾ teaspoon cumin seeds

Place all ingredients into a food processor and mix together on low speed until barely smooth. If the coconut is old, the mixture may turn out too dry; add 1 tablespoon lemon juice or water to mix and continue processing to correct this.

MAKES ABOUT 1 CUP.

Note: For additional texture, stir in 1 tablespoon grated coconut and 2 tablespoons minced cilantro leaves after processing.

CILANTRO-LEMON OIL

I love using this oil in salad dressings, but it's also a winner when used to toss pasta, raw sunflower seeds, and a freshly grated, hard dry cheese like Parmesan. It imparts extra zest to homemade croutons (sprinkle on prior to baking), and serves as a delicious counterpoint to wafer-thin slices of red ripe tomatoes or raw onion and cucumber salad. The trick is to not overheat the canola oil; if it sizzles when a drop of water is added, remove pan from heat and let oil cool for 30 seconds or more before adding other ingredients (perform the sizzle test frequently during the cooling period).

¾ cup canola oil
¼ cup sesame oil
1 bunch cilantro (reserve 3 stems with leaves)
2 tablespoons grated fresh lemon zest
4 long thin strips fresh lemon peel

Slowly heat the canola oil in a medium saucepan over low heat until just before it sizzles, about 3 minutes, depending on the pan. Add the sesame oil, cilantro, and lemon zest. Stir gently. Remove from heat. Press the cilantro against bottom of pan with back of spoon, gently crushing leaves and releasing their natural oils. Cover the pan and let the oil mixture steep at room temperature for at least 8 hours, preferably overnight. Strain the oil into a sterilized glass bottle. Discard remaining cooked cilantro and lemon zest. Add fresh lemon peel and 3 cilantro stems with leaves to strained oil. Seal the bottle tightly and use when needed. If refrigerated, the oil will keep indefinitely, and will keep for about two weeks at room temperature if kept in a dark, cool place; make sure to let it warm to room temperature prior to use for maximum flavor.

MAKES ABOUT 1 CUP.

CILANTRO CHAMPAGNE

This nonalcoholic beverage is especially refreshing on hot summer days; its cool, light green color seems to soothe the palate as it's being poured into tall "highball" glasses or flutes. Hint: Processing the celery stalks and cilantro in a centrifugal or other type juicer eliminates unwanted pulp prior to whipping the drink in the blender, making for a smooth, light champagne. I do not recommend trying to make this drink exclusively in a blender, as the celery will string and the cilantro will not be processed enough for the desired consistency.

4 stalks celery
1 bunch cilantro
2 cups fresh pineapple juice
2 cups ice cubes
4 pineapple cubes
4 maraschino cherries
4 swizzle sticks

Process the celery stalks and cilantro in a juicer. Discard the pulp. Pour the liquid into a blender jar. Add the pineapple juice and ice cubes. Blend on high speed until smooth and frothy. Pour into tall beverage glasses. Spear one pineapple cube and one cherry on each swizzle stick. Place 1 garnished stick in each filled glass and serve immediately.

Makes 4 drinks.

CILANTRO ROUSER

This nutrient-rich, thick drink is a surefire morning eye-opener; if you want to eliminate some pulp, strain the liquid. I enjoy this garden-fresh beverage as a "liquid lunch" when I'm running short on time during the middle of the day; it takes only seconds to make and features many refrigerator staples. Vary vegetables according to season and taste, adding a beet and omitting the green bell pepper, for example. A centrifugal or other type juicer is a must here.

3 medium tomatoes, cut into quarters
2 bunches cilantro, separated into 6 equal portions
2 celery stalks
2 carrots, peeled
¼ green bell pepper, seeded
1 teaspoon salt (optional)
1 teaspoon sugar
¼ teaspoon freshly ground black pepper
1 teaspoon hot sauce (optional)

Alternately feed tomatoes and cilantro sprigs through juicer, following with celery stalks, carrots, and green bell pepper. Add salt, sugar, black pepper, and hot sauce. Stir well and serve.

MAKES ABOUT 4 SERVINGS.

CORIANDER-CORNMEAL WAFFLES WITH CACTUS PEAR SYRUP

This breakfast favorite wins raves from all my overnight guests. Cactus pear syrup is made from the sweet red fruit of the prickly pear cactus and is available throughout the Southwest, in Latin specialty-food markets, or via mail order. Each season, I must race to harvest the delicious globes from the cactus around my home, as they're a highly sought-after sweet prized by the local *javelina* (wild boar), raccoons, and ring-tailed cats. When the wildlife beats me to the pears, I've found that strawberry syrup makes a successful substitute.

Waffles:
3 tablespoons unsalted butter, softened
2 tablespoons sugar
3 eggs
1 ½ cups milk
2 tablespoons baking powder
½ teaspoon salt
1 tablespoon freshly grated lemon zest
1 ½ cups cornmeal
¾ cup whole wheat flour
1 cup cilantro leaves, minced

Syrup:
8 ruby-red, ripe prickly pears
(also known as cactus apples)
1 ½ cups sugar
1 tablespoon fresh lemon juice

If pears are still thorny, wear gloves and handle them with tongs. Use tweezers to remove all glocids (the spines) and rinse under rapidly running water. With especially tough spines, you may wish to use the tip of a paring knife to remove glocids at the base. Examine carefully to make sure all glocids are gone before processing for syrup. Place the pears in a deep pot and cover with water. Bring to a boil over high heat and let cook for 20 minutes, stirring occasionally. Drain off the water and discard. Mash the fruit thoroughly. Line a mesh strainer with cheesecloth and strain the pulp. Let the juice stand for 15 minutes after straining to settle the sediment. Slowly pour off the juice into a medium saucepan, being careful not to mix in the sediment. Discard the sediment. Add the sugar and lemon juice. Bring the pear mixture to a boil over medium-high heat, stirring frequently. Boil for 10 minutes, or until the syrup thickens. If the syrup is not thick enough, add 1 tablespoon of sugar at a time; if the syrup is too thick, add 1 tablespoon of water at a time. Remove from the heat and let cool. Reserve.

Preheat a waffle iron according to the manufacturer's directions. Beat together the butter and sugar on low speed until creamy. Add the eggs, milk, baking powder, salt, and lemon zest. Increase the beater speed to medium and beat the ingredients together for 1 minute. Slowly pour in the cornmeal and wheat flour and continue beating until well mixed. Set the beater speed to the lowest setting and add the cilantro leaves. Beat until just mixed. Pour the mixture onto the waffle iron and bake until waffles are light golden brown, according to manufacturer's directions. Remove the waffles to a warmed platter and serve immediately with syrup.

MAKES ABOUT 4 SERVINGS.

CILANTRO SALSA COCKTAIL

A juicer that removes virtually all pulp is indispensable here, as these unusual cocktails should be smooth as silk. If necessary, drain through a fine sieve until desired consistency is obtained. Some party animals may choose to add a dash of hot sauce with the lemon juice and liquor; this version is dubbed a "Hothead."

2 large green tomatoes
1 large cucumber, peeled
1 cup cilantro leaves, chopped
¼ cup fresh lemon juice
2 ounces tequila or vodka
Garnish:
2 celery spears with leaves on end

Blanch the tomatoes in boiling water for 2 minutes. Remove and let cool. Rub off the skins and discard. Cut the tomatoes into wedges; remove and discard the seeds. Cut the cucumber lengthwise; remove and discard the seeds. Juice tomatoes, cucumber, and cilantro in batches by alternating vegetables. Strain the liquid if necessary, discarding any solids. Stir in the lemon juice and liquor. Fill tall glasses halfway with ice. Pour in the beverage. Garnish with celery spears and serve immediately.

MAKES 2 COCKTAILS.

CILANTRO-SAGE CORN BREAD WITH SUN-DRIED TOMATO

Of all the corn bread recipes I've sampled throughout the Southwest, this is my absolute favorite. I've served it with soups and stews, steaming hot with jalapeño jelly on chilly winter mornings, even broken it up into a bowl of corn mole. Because this is a savory—not sweet—recipe, I don't recommend serving it with sugary fruit jellies or jams; instead, try slathering on cilantro or avocado butter.

1 ½ cups yellow cornmeal
½ cup whole wheat flour
1 tablespoon baking powder
1 teaspoon salt (not optional)
½ teaspoon dried sage
3 eggs
1 ¼ cups milk
½ cup minced cilantro leaves
¼ cup minced sun-dried tomatoes
1 tablespoon honey
¼ cup (½ stick) melted butter

Preheat oven to 400°F. Sift the cornmeal, wheat flour, baking powder, salt, and sage into a large bowl. Mix together the eggs, milk, cilantro, sun-dried tomatoes, and honey in a small bowl. Pour the egg mixture into the dry mixture and stir well. Pour over the melted butter and stir until thoroughly combined. Pour the batter into a

nonstick or buttered 9-inch-square baking pan. Place in the oven and bake for 18 to 20 minutes, or until a toothpick inserted in the center comes out clean and the top of the bread is lightly browned. Remove from oven and let cool for 15 minutes before serving.

MAKES 6 TO 8 LARGE SERVINGS.

CILANTRO-PIÑON STUFFING

Pine nuts (also known as *piñons*) are an ingredient that I harvest seasonally from trees on my property. Blue jays, ravens, ground squirrels, and other native wildlife also relish these tiny treats, so I am often forced to climb precariously in order to collect enough nut-filled pinecones for kitchen use. Of course, pine nuts are available with or without shells from supermarkets and health food stores, but that would take the fun out of it. Always purchase hulled nuts, as cracking the tough brown shells is very time-consuming and surprisingly messy (the nutmeats are incredibly tiny compared to their protective covering).

2 cups shelled pine nuts
⅓ cup melted butter
1 medium yellow onion, finely chopped
1 celery stalk, minced
4 cups coarse dry bread crumbs
1 cup chopped cilantro leaves
1 egg, lightly beaten
1 clove garlic, minced
1 tablespoon fresh lemon zest
1 teaspoon salt
½ teaspoon freshly ground black pepper
½ teaspoon dried sage
½ teaspoon dried thyme

Place the pine nuts in a dry skillet over medium-high heat and toast for 3 minutes, stirring constantly, or until the nuts turn light brown. Remove from the skillet and reserve. Melt the butter in the skillet over medium-high heat. Add the onions and sauté for 5 minutes, stirring occasionally. Add the pine nuts and remaining ingredients. Turn off the heat and stir vigorously for 30 seconds to combine well. Pour the mixture into a large bowl and toss well. Use as stuffing for turkey, chicken, or game birds.

MAKES APPROXIMATELY 6 CUPS, OR 8 TO 10 SERVINGS.

DESSERTS

CILANTRO-CITRUS FLUFF WITH MANGO AND PAPAYA

Timing is everything with this chilled summer dessert, so make sure you have no distractions while preparing it. Sweet, juicy tropical fruit is smothered in a light, airy foam resplendent with the cooling, lemony taste of fresh cilantro: Mmm!

Juice of 1 orange, about ¼ cup
¼ cup sugar
1 mango, peeled, seeded, and chopped into ½-inch cubes
1 papaya, peeled, seeded, and chopped into ½-inch cubes
½ cup cilantro leaves, finely chopped
One 3-ounce package lemon gelatin
½ cup water
2 tablespoons fresh-squeezed lemon juice
1 cup well-drained crushed ice (kept in freezer until needed)
12 cilantro leaves

Pour the orange juice into a small bowl. Pour the sugar into a second small bowl. Dip the rims of four margarita glasses quickly into the orange juice, then the sugar. Sugar crystals should cling to the rim of glasses and turn light orange. Place rimmed glasses in the freezer to chill for 5 minutes. When glasses are chilled, remove from freezer and portion the mango and papaya pieces into the glasses—carefully, so as not to dislodge any sugar crystals—and place in the refrigerator. Place the chopped cilantro leaves into a blender jar. Add the gelatin and reserve unblended. Combine the water

and lemon juice in a small pot and bring to a boil over high heat. Pour the boiling water mixture over the cilantro and gelatin. Cover the blender jar and process on high speed for 2 minutes to dissolve the gelatin. Remove the crushed ice from the freezer. While blender is running, slowly add crushed ice. Blend for 1 minute, or until the blender jar feels cold to the touch and the gelatin mixture is smooth and frothy. Remove the fruit-filled glasses from the refrigerator. Pour the gelatin mixture over the fruit. Return the filled glasses to refrigerator for 5 minutes. Remove glasses from refrigerator and garnish with 3 cilantro leaves each. Serve immediately.

MAKES 4 SERVINGS.

HISTORIC CORIANDER COOKIES

Coriander seed has been a valued culinary ingredient for over five thousand years; in Revolutionary War times, colonial American cooks made a stiff cookie dough from soured milk that prominently featured this pungent spice. Various versions of the recipe featured below date back to the westward expansion, having been passed down from generation to generation of settlers, and eventually became part of Arizona's culinary heritage. While delicious plain, these cookies are especially nice with a bit of white icing.

½ cup vegetable shortening
6 teaspoons ground coriander seeds
½ teaspoon salt
¼ teaspoon baking soda
1 cup sugar
1 large egg
1 cup flour
¼ cup buttermilk
1 cup flour
¼ cup buttermilk

Preheat oven to 375°F. Combine the shortening, coriander, salt, and baking soda in a large mixing bowl. Beat together at low speed, adding in the sugar slowly. Add the

egg and the first cup of flour. Keep beating. Add ¼ cup buttermilk and the second cup of flour. Keep beating, adding the last ¼ cup of buttermilk slowly. Beat until well blended. Drop teaspoons of dough 2 inches apart onto a nonstick cookie sheet. Bake the cookies for 12 to 15 minutes, or until lightly browned around edges. Remove from the oven and let cool.

MAKES APPROXIMATELY 36 COOKIES.

CILANTRO-LIME GRANITA

Make up this refreshing recipe at least 24 hours in advance; it's worth waiting for! The crisp, clean flavor makes this frozen ice a wonderful between-courses palate cleanser, but when garnished with fresh raspberries or cantaloupe balls, it becomes an irresistible dessert.

3 cups water
2 cups sugar
1 bunch cilantro, chopped
½ cup fresh lime juice
2 tablespoons finely grated lime zest
4 cups crushed ice cubes
Garnish:
Cilantro sprigs
Red raspberries

Combine the water, sugar, cilantro, lime juice, and zest in a large saucepan over high heat. Bring to a boil and cook for 30 minutes, stirring frequently. Remove from the heat and let cool. Drain the liquid and reserve, discarding the solids. Pour the liquid into a nonreactive container and cover. Place the covered container in the freezer and leave for 24 hours. The mixture will not freeze solid but will appear slushy. Remove the slush from the freezer and spoon into a blender jar. Process at medium speed, adding crushed ice 1 cup at a time, until mixture is icy and all cubes are finely crushed. Portion into four tall parfait glasses and garnish with cilantro sprigs and berries. Serve immediately.

MAKES 4 SERVINGS.

CILANTRO-ORANGE SORBET

Liqueur sorbets make the perfect ending to an elegant dinner party. Instead of emphasizing cilantro's natural zest with lemon or lime juice, this recipe presents a titillating counterpoint through fresh orange juice and Grand Marnier, an orange-flavored liqueur highly prized by professional pastry chefs. This recipe should be made up at least 8 hours in advance.

1 ½ cups sugar
3 ½ cups water
1 cup chopped cilantro
Zest of 2 oranges, finely grated
Juice of 2 oranges, about ½ cup
2 ½ ounces Grand Marnier liqueur, about ⅓ cup
1 egg white
Garnish:
Candied orange peel
Cilantro sprigs

Combine the sugar, water, and cilantro in a large saucepan over high heat. Bring to a boil and cook for 5 minutes, stirring frequently. Stir in the orange zest and juice and liqueur. Remove from heat and let steep for 30 minutes. Strain the liquid and discard the solids. Pour into a nonreactive container and cover. Place the covered container in freezer and leave for 2 hours. Beat the egg white slightly and stir into the chilled mixture. Cover the mixture and return to the freezer for 6 hours. Stir the mixture and spoon into serving dishes. Garnish with orange peel and cilantro sprigs. Serve immediately.

MAKES 6 SERVINGS.

INDEX

A

B

C

ABOUT THE AUTHOR

P. J. Birosik is food editor of the *Sedona Red Rock News*, and credits her salsa savvy to summers spent sampling Tex-Mex cuisine in Ft. Stockston, Texas, during her childhood and teenage years, and numerous vacations in Baja California and mainland Mexico. She is the author of several books including *The Burrito Book*, *Salsa*, and *The New Age Music Guide*. She frequently writes on organic gardening, healthy snack foods, and all-natural cooking for numerous publications including *Whole Life Times* and *Yoga Journal* and is listed in *Who's Who Among Women* and *Who's Who in the West*. P. J. Birosik lives in Sedona, Arizona.

≺ Back Cover

1. Corn-and-Coriander-Stuffed Pork Chops
2. Tucson Tabbouleh Salad
3. Chilled Fajita Salad

Inside Back Cover ➤

1. El Paso Pesto with Linguine, Caviar, and Chevre
2. Creamy Carrot-Cilantro Salad
3. Lamb Chops with Cilantro-Parmesan Spread